SHAKESPEAREAN STRUCTURES

SHAKESPEAREAN STRUCTURES

Ralph Berry

BARNES & NOBLE BOOKS
TOTOWA, NEW JERSEY

First Published in the U.S.A. 1981 by
BARNES & NOBLE BOOKS
81, Adams Drive, Totowa,
New Jersey, 07512

ISBN 0–389–20173–1

Printed in Hong Kong

FOR MARY AND MARCUS

Contents

Preface

This book is a collection of discrete essays on Shakespeare. Its unity is that of my interests, which are those of form and language. I look above all for a major structuring strategy, and with Shakespeare one always finds a principle of order that expresses itself in a multitude of ways. Through analysis of situation—as, here, in *Othello*—one discovers that everyone in the play is undergoing a variant of the same experience, helping to parse the same concepts. The ensemble of acting is reflected back into the text, which presents a repertory of dramatis personæ going about its business of presenting a unitary experience.

The essays here follow the chronology of the canon. They move from the more primitive, and easily legible, experiments of the early Shakespeare to the masterly intuitions of *The Winter's Tale*. *2 Henry VI* exploits a single dominant metaphor, the Trial, which provides a rigid vertebrate structure for the drama. Women, in the early plays, I see as conveying a critique of the central transactions. These somewhat stiff and angular strokes of construction yield to the subtler, more diffused methods of the mature Shakespeare. Everyone is familiar with Shakespeare's handling of the dual location system, as twin repositories of values. In *Hamlet*, I show how the symbolic geography of six nations composes a rough mosaic of Hamlet's mind. In *Measure for Measure*, I view the dual location as vertical. The social and topographic echelons of Vienna figure the recesses and open spaces of the mind, its cellars and high public balconies. *Measure for Measure* proposes that the roots of action are sexual. A variant of the same idea informs the archetypal action of *Macbeth*. The killing of Duncan is, at the point of decision, a sexual temptation and a sexual choice. With *Timon of Athens*, the keystone of structure is marked by what technically has to be regarded as wordplay. *Leech*, in Alcibiades' final "Prescribe to other, as each other's leech", combines two separate lines of imagistic development, those of bloodsucking (eating) and bloodletting (healing). The elegant stereoscoping of terms is Shakespeare's solution to the philosophic antitheses of the play.

Finally, in *The Winter's Tale*, I return to the controlling metaphor, now a far more delicate and complex affair, which expresses the ordering principle of Time: Time as dance, Time as wave, that pulses through the action. In the end one needs metaphors to elucidate Shakespeare, and they are his primary structures.

R.B.

Acknowledgements

An earlier version of Chapter 5, "Pattern in *Othello*", appeared in *Shakespeare Quarterly*. Chapters 3 and 4, on *Hamlet* and *Measure for Measure*, were published in *University of Toronto Quarterly;* Chapter 2, "Woman as Fool", appeared in *Dalhousie Review*. I am grateful to the University of Toronto Press, and the Editors of *University of Toronto Quarterly*, *Shakespeare Quarterly*, and *Dalhousie Review* for their permission to reprint this material.

R.B.

I *2 Henry VI:* Trial by Combat

A single metaphoric envelope encases *2 Henry VI*, the Trial. We need the concept, for criticism has done only partial justice to the unity of the play. It is not that there is substantial disagreement concerning the general import of *2 Henry VI*. Even today, Tillyard's account is not I think in serious dispute. For him, the play's action is a series of offences against order, with Iden the prime symbol of degree. "I seek not to wax great by others' waning" (IV, x, 22). "The central theme then is political intrigue";[1] and J. P. Brockbank's phrase, "The Frame of Disorder", sums up the usual view. But the unity of *2 Henry VI* is accepted only with some reservation. Tillyard saw it as "very well plotted . . .", even "perhaps the most harmonious play in the tetralogy".[2] Since intrigue and dissension are the substance of the entire play, he argued that the scenes of Horner, the pirates, Cade and so on, "at first sign episodic, are greatly to the point".[3] A. S. Cairncross, in his New Arden edition, justified the lesser events more cautiously, and on broader grounds:

> Both for filling out his "cast," and for variety of incident and flexibility of staging, Shakespeare felt it necessary to add a number of subsidiary events that lay scattered and often irrelevant about the chronicles. Such are the Armourer scenes, the conjuring, Iden's triumph, and the miracle of St. Albans.[4]

And Irving Ribner, coupling Part Two with the other plays in the trilogy, had considerable reservations concerning Shakespeare's construction:

> With so wide a scope, so many dramatic purposes to accomplish, it is almost inevitable that all three of the *Henry VI* plays should be episodic in structure; scenes are often poorly related to one another, and what unity the plays possess is that implicit in a

theme of general disorder and chaos brought about by treachery and self-seeking on the part of nobles who should instead be devoted entirely to the good of England.[5]

"Episodic" is the word we have to take note of. It implies a lack of connection between the parts and the whole, or a connection discernible on the broadest of grounds only. And this, naturally, is the critical challenge. The assumption must always be that a Shakespeare play is a unity, which can be apprehended and described in a number of ways. The major problem is to detect the central principle of organization, and relate it to the play's action, throughout the major and minor episodes. I propose here a more exact account of the organization and action of *2 Henry VI*. Its essential form is that of the Trial. The processes of a Trial—charges, investigation, arraignment, defence, verdict, sentence, and execution —compose the pattern that orders *2 Henry VI*.

I

The opening event of the play—the announcement of the articles negotiated between France and England—sets in motion the first exchange of charges. To Humphrey, Duke of Gloucester, Suffolk has given away Anjou and Maine : to the Cardinal of Winchester, Gloucester seeks to advance the one step beyond Protector : "I fear me, lords, for all this flattering gloss. / He will be found a dangerous Protector" (I, i, 163–4). Dramatically—not formally—Gloucester is defended by Salisbury, the rest having departed : "I never saw but Humphrey Duke of Gloucester / Did bear him like a noble gentleman" (I, i, 183–4). The opening scene yields to the preparation for a future trial : the agent provocateur, Hume, discloses the plot of Suffolk and the Cardinal to incriminate the Protector's wife. "And her attainture will be Humphrey's fall" (I, ii, 106). I, iii presents certain petitions, a mutation of charges. The Petitioners accidentally disclose their complaints (against Suffolk, and the Cardinal) to Suffolk, not the Protector. Peter, the Armourer's man then lays charges against his master :

Second Petitioner   Alas, Sir, I am but a poor petitioner of our whole township.

Peter [*presents his petition*] Against my master, Thomas Horner, for saying that the Duke of York was rightful heir to the crown.
Queen   What say'st thou? Did the Duke of York say he was rightful heir to the crown?
Peter   That my master was? No, forsooth! My master said that he was, and that the king was an usurper.

(I, iii, 26–34)

We do not know the truth of the matter at this point, and Peter is remanded for questioning. The episode is the first of the series in which the activities of the lesser sort echo—and thus, mock—those of the mighty. These we return to, with Suffolk's accusations (augmented by the Cardinal, Somerset, Buckingham and the Queen) against Gloucester. "Since thou wert king (as who is king but thou?) / The commonwealth hath daily run to wrack", and so on (I, iii, 126–40). Gloucester's answer states a fundamental value: "Prove them, and I lie open to the law" (I, iii, 159).

The mighty's connection with the humble is an actual, as well as a formal relationship. Horner the Armourer and Peter now enter; Suffolk seeks to exploit his windfall and turn Peter's evidence against York. "Because here is a man accus'd of treason: / Pray God the Duke of York excuse himself!" (I, iii, 180–1). Peter stands by his claim; York denounces Horner for a traitor; the Armourer asserts that this is a matter of a malevolent apprentice. What is the truth? Henry puts the problem to Gloucester: "Uncle, what shall we say to this in law?" (I, iii, 207). That is Henry's question, and the play's question. Duke Humphrey's answer is the play's answer:

> And let these have a day appointed them
> For single combat in convenient place,
> For he hath witness of his servant's malice:
> This is the law, and this Duke Humphrey's doom.

(I, iii, 211–14)

The processes of the Law acknowledge themselves, in effect, inadequate to sift the truth and arrive at a judgment. The matter is to be left to God: and the stronger sword. It is curious that the modern sense of "doom" yields a superior meaning to the final line; for Duke Humphrey's verdict becomes the fate that the play imposes on him.

II

There follows the triumph of the agents provocateurs (I, iv); the conjuring, so far from irrelevance, is dramatized evidence at the trial of Eleanor. The movement of the play is now from charges to trials—that is, the business of testing charges. Following the emblematic falcon-passage ("Yea, man and birds are fain of climbing high", II, i, 8) occurs another flurry of noble bickering; and this time the matter is put to a variant of trial-by-combat, the duel. The Cardinal suggests, and the Protector accepts, an encounter "on the east side of the grove" (II, i, 43). The episode contains its own judgment. All the decency, and justice, of Duke Humphrey comes down to "Now, by God's mother, priest, I'll shave your crown for this, / Or all my fence shall fail" (II, i, 51–2).

The episode is really of formal interest: the part reflects the whole, but is itself entirely dispensable, for the duel does not take place. The case of Saunder Simpcox supervenes; and now the duellist becomes the Public Prosecutor, who in masterly style probes a case of suspected fraud before himself administering justice. The vein is comic, as these parodies of major concerns normally are in Shakespeare. Yet the pain of Henry is the play's, and ours: "Oh God, seest Thou this, and bearest so long?" (II, i, 153).[6] And scarcely has Gloucester given judgment on Simpcox and his wife, "Let them be whipped through every market town till they come to Berwick, from whence they came" (II, i, 158–60) than Buckingham enters, with news of the arraignment of Eleanor. Humphrey, too, will be punished with his wife. The scene ends with the sombre, ineffectual words of a failing judiciary:

> *King*   Tomorrow toward London back again,
> To look into this business thoroughly
> And call these foul offenders to their answers
> And poise the cause in justice' equal scales,
> Whose beam stands sure, whose rightful cause prevails.
>
> (II, i, 201–5)

The discussion between York, Salisbury, and Warwick (II, ii) is an interlude, if you like: its tone is even, the matter dry, even boring, But it is perfectly apt to the play's concerns. I liken it to the taking of Counsel's opinion in chambers. That, indeed, is virtually how York puts it, in the scene's opening lines:

Now, my good Lords of Salisbury and Warwick,
Our simple supper ended, give me leave
In this close walk to satisfy myself,
In craving your opinion of my title,
Which is infallible, to England's crown.

(II, ii, 1–5)

The matter is legal, and necessarily so. York wishes to have it confirmed that he has a cast-iron case, before he proceeds further. His backers agree entirely. "What plain proceeding is more plain than this?" (II, ii, 53). Thus, the Civil Wars themselves become a larger form of trial: legality, and with it morality, pronounces a shrewd case against the king.

The play's single formal Trial, however, is that of Eleanor. II, iii exhibits its conclusion :

King   Stand forth, Dame Eleanor Cobham, Gloucester's wife :
In sight of God and us, your guilt is great :
Receive the sentence of the law for sins
Such as are by God's book adjudg'd to death.

(II, iii, 1–4)

Her guilt is real enough—the play has demonstrated that fully—still, the evidence for the trial has been procured by the most questionable of means. An unemphasized irony is that Hume, who set the case up against Eleanor, is himself condemned to death. From this flawed justice we move to a parallel form, the trial by combat. The cross-charges of Horner and his man, Peter, are resolved by single combat. Now this incident is in Hall : and yet as presented by Shakespeare it takes on a different aspect. It is not simply a matter of contributing to the play's variations of trial. It is rather that this episode seems a central referent to the play. For what is the larger action, but a Trial by Combat? And what is the smaller episode, but a grimace at the outcome of the Wars? Peter emerges the winner, but only because his master is too drunk to defend himself. Thus he dies, confessing treason. Peter's view of the matter is predictable : "O God, have I overcome mine enemies in this presence? O Peter, thou has prevailed in right !" (II, iii, 101–2). So is the king's :

> Go, take hence that traitor from our sight;
> For by his death we do perceive his guilt :
> And God in justice hath reveal'd to us
> The truth and innocence of this poor fellow,
> Which he had thought to have murder'd wrongfully.
>
> (ii, iii, 103–7)

I put it that the play does not invite us to share the view of Divine Providence advanced by Peter and King Henry.

The "right" that Peter recognizes does not save Duke Humphrey. His arraignment is presented in iii, i. A series of accusations culminates in Suffolk's "I do arrest thee of high treason here" (iii, i, 97). Charges—but no evidence—are brought against Humphrey, himself the play's main spokesman for the Law. The central Act is in every way a legal travesty. Humphrey defends himself skilfully, but unavailingly; nameless "mightier crimes" (iii, i, 134) are to be urged against him, and Henry permits the Duke to be led away to captivity, there to await a formal trial. The scene's perversion of justice reaches its climax with the agreement among the Queen, Suffolk, York and the Cardinal to have Humphrey put to death. This is justified by Suffolk's remarkable argument that Gloucester's essential guilt stands in no need of confirmation through the tiresome legalisms of a trial :

> Madam, 'tis true; and were't not madness then,
> To make the fox surveyor of the fold?
> Who being accus'd a crafty murderer,
> His guilt should be but idly posted over
> Because his purpose is not executed.
> No, let him die in that he is a fox,
> By nature prov'd an enemy to the flock,
> Before his chaps be stain'd with crimson blood,
> As Humphrey, prov'd by treasons, to my liege.
>
> (iii, i, 252–60)

III

And so Humphrey, Duke of Gloucester, is condemned to death. It is trial by accusation, leading to a quasi-judicial murder. His death becomes the new fact to which the play is subdued; and Warwick becomes, in effect, the investigator of the crime. The marvellously observed detail of his long speech ("See, how the blood is settled in his face", III, ii, 160–78) is that of an accomplished criminal investigator. There is no escaping his conclusion: "It cannot be but he was murd'red here; / The least of all these signs were probable" (III, ii, 177–8). Warwick, proceeding from the strongest of circumstantial evidence, then lays charges against Suffolk. And Henry, with the Commons in uproar to spur him on, pronounces the sentence of banishment that is Suffolk's fate. A kind of justice emerges from all this: even so, the murder of Duke Humphrey is alone sufficient to invest with a savage irony the commentary of King Henry—lines which, quoted out of their context, are normally curtailed of their resonance:

> Thrice is he arm'd that hath his quarrel just,
> And he but naked, though lock'd up in steel,
> Whose conscience with injustice is corrupted.
>
> (III, ii, 233–5)

The close relationship between these events and the formal processes of Law is marked. Moreover, the experience of one aspect of a trial—the preceding examination—is finely evoked in the death scene of the Cardinal. The language of his dying cries ("reason in madness", as the technique became in *King Lear*) places with great exactness the emotional situation of the guilt-ridden Cardinal:

> Bring me unto my trial when you will.
> Died he not in his bed? where should he die?
> Can I make men live, whe'r they will or no?
> O, torture me no more! I will confess.
> Alive again? Then show me where he is.
> I'll give a thousand pound to look upon him.
> He hath no eyes, the dust hath blinded them.
> Comb down his hair; look, look! it stands upright,
> Like lime-twigs set to catch my winged soul.
> Give me some drink; and bid the apothecary
> Bring the strong poison that I bought of him.
>
> (III, iii, 8–18)

It is an examination. The prisoner has broken down under the rigours of the interrogation. Under torture, the prisoner confesses his crime, and asks only for some drink—and his own release through death. This, a moment later, the Cardinal achieves. The dramatic point of the scene is that Winchester's assumed fate is damnation. Called upon to raise his hand as a sign of hope in Heaven's mercy, he fails to do so. "He dies, and makes no sign" (III, iii, 29). Thus another kind of sentence has been passed. Henry's comment is permitted to close the scene: "Forbear to judge, for we are sinners all" (III, iii, 31).

This movement of the play ends with the death of Suffolk. It is not presented as a mere bloody scuffle over a long-boat's side. The sailors, savage though they are, are prepared to ransom a gentleman. But Suffolk, his identity disclosed, is different. His nemesis is now the Lieutenant. This nameless man rehearses the catalogue of Suffolk's crimes against the realm; and in the name of that realm pronounces sentence upon Suffolk. "Ay, kennel, puddle, sink! whose filth and dirt / Troubles the silver spring where England drinks", etc. (IV, i, 71–193). The Lieutenant, now Judge, speaks for England. His verdict has the ring of dignity and truth, an unchallengeable decorum. Suffolk's execution is wholly justified. Yet again, the impact of the action is that of a Trial.

IV

Suffolk dead, Act IV concerns itself entirely with the Cade rebellion. This—the most important minor action of the play, a self-contained sub-plot—has of course the general function of mimicking the activities of the great. (Cade's pretensions to lineage, for instance— IV, ii, 41–52—are deplorably similar to the claims of York, whose tool he is.) We need not look closely at the Cade scenes as a whole here. But some of the episodes are interesting as further contributions to the dramatic design we consider. Yet another judicial enquiry is presented: Cade examines the Clerk of Chartham. He, it appears, is charged with reading and writing, to say nothing of arithmetic. "Come hither, sirrah, I must examine thee", says Cade (IV, ii, 104). The matter is abbreviated by a timely confession. "Sir, I thank God, I have been so well brought up that I can write my name": at which the crowd choruses, "He hath confessed. Away with him! He's a villain and a traitor" (IV, ii, 112–15). (Just as "traitor" is the archetypal charge in this play, the peremptory "away"—e.g., I, iii, 223; IV, i, 103—signals the dismissal of the prisoner.) The popular verdict being confirmed by the tribune of the people, the Clerk is led out to summary execution. The funny-horrible tone of this encounter is repeated in the later trial of Lord Say.[7] He has to face the (standard radical) charge, of having "most traitorously corrupted the youth of the realm in erecting a grammar school" (IV, vii, 34–5). For this, and other offences against the realm, he is condemned to death. This macabre caricature of a Court of Law, Goyaesque in tone, is at once a statement of England's disorder and a covert reminder that his betters (Suffolk, the Cardinal, and York, in III, i) did not employ notably superior judicial methods.

Evidently, the Cade scenes extend further the fabric of which the play is constructed, while permitting a complete contrast of mood and personnel. The fate of Cade, moreover, is settled on the same basis as virtually everyone else's in *2 Henry VI*. Brought to bay in Iden's orchard, the rebel falls to the sword of that celebrated symbol of degree, Iden. The victory of right is not, however, presented as being determined by moral factors. Cade himself, as he emphasizes—and Iden confirms—is starving. There is no reason to doubt Cade's dying claim that "Famine and no other hath slain me" (IV, x, 65). This (in effect) trial-by-combat makes a laconic point similar to its fellow in II, iii. Just as a drunk is unlikely to beat a man in full possession of his few wits, so a starving man is at a disadvantage in combat with a well-fed—and well-built—opponent.

V

An attitude of detached and sceptical irony is seen to control the events of the final Act. The cycle appears to have turned fully, for the play returns to the situation of charges and counter-charges. In the fresh outburst of accusations, York impeaches Henry:

> King did I call thee? No, thou art not king,
> Not fit to govern and rule multitudes,
> Which dar'st not, no nor canst not rule a traitor.

(V, i, 93–5)

Somerset, supported by Clifford, charges York with treason:

> O monstrous traitor! I arrest thee, York,
> Of capital treason 'gainst the king and crown,
> (v, i, 106–7)

Yet the repetition is with a difference. The apparent return to the situation of Act I marks the intensified convulsions of the land. And the elements of right and morality, bearing with them the hope and expectation of the audience, have all but vanished from the play. Henry, supported by his discredited Queen, the haughty Somerset, and Clifford, is left to make good his belief that "Thrice is he armed that hath his quarrel just". Against him are ranged Warwick, the good old Salisbury, and the insanely ambitious York. It is impossible to feel that either alliance has more than a partial claim to right; only the formal claims are left. The audience feels, and is meant to feel, an impulse of rejection that it did not earlier experience. The outcome of their contest is therefore seen as a victory for the stronger. It is no less, and it cannot be more.

The battle of St. Albans is, then, a true climax to the play: it embodies perfectly the movements and situations we have considered. (Even the place of battle recalls the earlier, hollow Miracle.) What is at stake is a Trial, for both sides claim to be the keepers of right and justice. The matter is formalized in the encounter between Clifford and York, York making the claim that all the combatants share:

> So let it help me now against thy sword
> As I in justice and true right express it.
> (v, ii, 24–5)

"Justice", "right": at some time or other virtually everyone who has taken significant part in the drama has related his actions to these concepts. But the resolution of these claims is ultimately a trial of strength. St. Albans, that oddly flat climax, is a—necessarily tautological—demonstration that the stronger side defeats the weaker. It is appropriate, then, for the dying Clifford to murmur *"La fin couronne les oeuvres"* (v, ii, 28), and for Warwick to end the play with the hollow rhetoric of:

Now, by my faith, lords, 'twas a glorious day:
Saint Alban's battle won by famous York
Shall be eterniz'd in all age to come.
Sound drum and trumpets, and to London all;
And more such days as there to us befall!

(v, iii, 29–33)

The organizing metaphor of *2 Henry VI*, as I discern it, is that of a Trial. At bottom, this play is constructed (as, given its material, it must be) on a simple binary principle, the opposition of contending forces. But the dramatic form that this construction takes relates the events to the processes of a Court of Law. In part, this is the manifest content of the play (the trial of Eleanor, the Peter–Horner encounter): but generally the situations are quasi-judicial, as in the arraignment of Humphrey, the examinations of Lord Say and the Clerk of Chartham, the investigations of Simpcox's miracle and Humphrey's death. The language often draws attention to the dramatic relevance of the situation: this is especially true of the Cardinal's death-bed scene (a confession, in effect, under interrogation), and of the Lieutenant's sentence upon Suffolk. The Trial is the grand image of *2 Henry VI*. And it becomes a kind of **metaphor** for the renewed outbreak of the Civil Wars in Act v. Certainly, the language of the combatants—the appeals to "justice" and "right", coupled with denunciation of the opposition as "traitors"—continue to evoke in us the awareness of the central dramatic image. And the outcome of this form of trial is merely a variant of the earlier miniature, the encounter between Horner and Peter. The part gives the vital clue to the whole; we can regard the battle of St. Albans, and the entire play, as a Trial-by-Combat.

2 Woman as Fool: Dramatic Mechanism in Shakespeare

"Don't ask what it means, ask what it does" ran the Cambridge injunction: the linguistic precept helps us to re-open the question of women's status in Shakespeare. A direct assault on meaning, via an assessment of female character as portrayed in the plays, is evidently primitive. A more refined version of the old-style approach through character is to regard stage women as embodying or suggesting certain contemporary controversies.[1] However suggestive and rewarding, this approach does court the ontological trap of assuming "women" to be invariably equivalent to a "female character in a play". Clearly, on many occasions we (and the audience) can assume a close correspondence between *woman* and the fictive image. After all, a basic point in having female characters on stage is that they remind the audience of women off-stage. So a female character, addressing herself to matters of directly sexual interest—marriage, the importunacies of city gallants, the legal position of Elizabethan women—evokes a strong audience reaction through the allusion to contemporary life. But that is not the sole, or even necessarily a major, reason for the dramatic existence of women. The needs of stagecraft go beyond straight reportage of women, as perceived by the dramatist. It would be tediously pedantic to insist on referring to "female character" throughout this essay; but I emphasize that "woman" is purely a convention of discourse. I want here to view the matter as a dramatic mechanism. That is, I suggest that we ask: what, in the context of the total play, is Shakespeare using women *for*?

A part, undoubtedly, of a proper response is to resist the question. One can maintain that at all times Shakespeare is depicting human beings, not deploying a set of cardboards as agents; and I agree that it would be absurd to speak of "using" Cleopatra, or Juliet, or Rosalind. The female character is totally assimilated into the play's design; is subject and mechanism combined. Still, we start from the iron premise that Shakespeare is at all times a dramatist, whose objectives are subdued to the needs of each dramatic enterprise. That enterprise will create its own dramatic laws, its own problems and solutions. A design concerned with high politics, and therefore with men, may need women simply to throw light on the domestic side of their menfolk. Lady Percy, Portia, and Calpurnia exist because of Hotspur, Brutus, and Caesar. A design concentrated upon a major relationship—*The Taming of the Shrew, Antony and Cleopatra*—needs the woman for exactly the same reason as it needs the man: you need two people to make a relationship. A design composed around a central figure, but recognizing the most important of the radial relationships, must calculate Lady Macbeth in relation to her husband. Stage women have diverse functions to perform, not easily subject to generalization. Nevertheless, a certain sense of the strategic utility of women does, I think, emerge in the early plays of Shakespeare. Those plays are constructed with a clear architectural line, around which the scaffolding is still visible; and for these, my question retains its point. In those early plays we recognize a design in which women have a clear function in locating, and stating the thesis of the drama.

Every play in the canon consists (as in historical context it must) in its broadest formulation, of a largely male cast, usually making a botch of affairs. Now how is this situation to be analysed and expounded? The solution requires an impulse of challenge and intelligence to be directed at the inadequacies of the central transactions. This critical intelligence can come from several quarters on stage. In the histories, the French—whose status is that of opponents and foils to the English—often supply a challenge in the cross-Channel manoeuvrings. But for obvious reasons of audience response, the French cannot be built up too far as refuters of the English. Again, the rebels in *Henry IV* supply a challenge; and for equally obvious reasons of ideology and dramatic design, Hotspur and company are depicted as lightweights, and losers. These are local factors in a local dramatic problem. Sometimes a high-ranking subordinate supplies this impulse: the Lord Chief Justice, Kent, Enorbarbus, Camillo. The two great sources of critical challenge, however, are the Fools; and women.

Intelligence without power is what they have in common. I have proposed elsewhere[2] that the function of clowns (and rustics, servants, plebeians) in Shakespeare is to amplify the ancient role of jester: they mock authority; and in mocking it, they reveal its limitations. This is true whether the jester figure is himself a person of intelligence (Speed, Touchstone), or, bucolically, constitutes a parodic comment on his betters (Bottom, Dogberry). The use of social inferiors to comment, directly or obliquely, on the actions of the great is a constant resource of Shakespeare's stagecraft: it runs from the Dromios of Ephesus and Syracuse, through Michael Williams' challenge to Henry V and the servants' dialogue in Act IV of *Coriolanus,* to the burlesque conspiracy of Stephano and Trinculo. It is, however, narrowly true that the terminus of the intelligent jester line is the Fool in *King Lear.*

With the Fools come, in natural alliance, women. This is a structural formation, but sometimes becomes an on-stage pairing. Costard gets on well with the ladies of the Court, and the Princess is especially gracious to him at the pageant of Worthies; Touchstone accompanies Celia and Rosalind into exile; Viola and Feste strike up a guarded understanding (*Twelfth Night,* III, i). The immediate mechanics of stage presentation are not worth pursuing here, though it is important to note that women and Fools are never, prior to *King Lear,* in major contention. There is a natural affinity, but not an identity between the perspective of each group. Generally, a Fool is well placed to point out that his master is behaving stupidly (Speed on Valentine) or that the values of the entire society are deficient (Touchstone on the "sport" of wrestling at Duke Frederick's court). But the women argue, more cogently, from a single point of reference: themselves.

That is why the clearest instances of woman-as-Intelligence come in the early comedies, and why it is unnecessary to linger long over them. The plot is courtship, and the issue is acceptance. The women are, so to speak, necessarily women; their sexual situation is the plot. The mechanism is detailed, once and for all, in *Love's Labour Lost,* where four women confront four male wooers, and arrive eventually at the terms on which the sexual settlement is made. Certain points emerge with great clarity from this exemplary play. First, the individuals are manifestly units in a sexual group. Individual characteristics are observable in all eight—even with Dumaine and Maria there is something for the actor and actress to seize on—still, we recognize what is in essence a male *v.* female joust. Second, the female group expresses the Intelligence of the play. It is important to note that this has nothing to do with individual intelligence. Berowne is highly intelligent, not less so than

Rosaline, but his cleverness is a mask for folly. The play endorses the final negotiating position of the women, that the male oaths must be tested against a year's probation. And this Intelligence takes on often the mode of a philosophical enquiry. The women, in the masque encounter especially, appear as philosophy dons analysing and refuting the erroneous propositions of sophomores.

Love's Labour's Lost is a demonstration play, and its lessons are applicable to *The Two Gentlemen of Verona*. The dramaturgic limitation is that the women, in expressing Intelligence, express also a direct self-interest. Of greater resonance are the occasions when the Intelligence is not identical with a simple concern with self. I instance two of the early histories: *I Henry VI*, and *Richard III*.

I Henry VI is not a primitive play, but a play about primitives. The impulse of the dramatist is not merely to chronicle the English decline in France—mournfully, though with intellectual neutrality —but to identify the causality of the affair. The root of the matter is the dissension and mental limitations of the English nobles; and this is pointed out through the choric commentaries of the Messenger, Exeter, the Mayor of London, and others. There is however a subtler critique of the English governing group. It is presented, first, through the Talbot–Countess of Auvergne interlude, the "peaceful comic sport" as Burgundy calls it (II, ii, 45).

It is the first instance in Shakespeare of the "stalking horse" technique, which I suppose most of us know best as a standard Shavian resource. In this, the dramatist presents a persuasive and logical argument through the mouth of a character whom the audience is conditioned to detest. (Cf. Shylock, and Undershaft the arms manufacturer in *Major Barbara*.) The Countess of Auvergne is French; and bent on treachery towards Talbot, whom generations of commentators used to assume to be the "hero" of *I Henry VI*.[3] Prepare, then, to hiss a Gallic Judith. Her charge against Talbot, though, sounds unpleasantly convincing:

> That hast by tyranny these many years
> Wasted our country, slain our citizens
> And sent our sons and husbands captivate.
>
> (II, iii, 40–2)

It is perfectly true. What is the case for the English being in France, a presence that history had decisively resolved by the time of this play? It is never argued, merely asserted:[4]

> These are his substance, sinews, arms and strength,
> With which he yoketh your rebellious necks,
> Razeth your cities and subverts your towns
> And in a moment makes them desolate.
>
> (II, iii, 63–6)

says Talbot, pointing to his soldiers. For the moment, the argument is conclusive. Might is right, and Talbot has it. And what happens when Talbot runs out of soldiers? The play leaves the question hanging in the air. One scarcely needs superhuman perception to detect it. Talbot encounters, in Act IV, the fate that is latent in his response to the Countess of Auvergne. The real challenge to the representative Englishman is, why should the English be fighting in France? And it is posed, obliquely, by a woman.

Still more interesting is Shakespeare's exploitation of Pucelle. She conforms in the main to audience preconceptions—treacherous, a witch, the Dauphin's trull. All the greater, therefore, is the explosive force of the surprise Shakespeare detonates in IV, vii. To Lucy's:

> But where's the great Alcides of the field,
> Valiant Lord Talbot, Earl of Shrewsbury,
> Created, for his rare success in arms,
> Great Earl of Washford, Waterford, and Valence;
> Lord Talbot of Goodrig and Urchinfield,
> Lord Strange of Blackmere, Lord Verdun of Alton,
> Lord Cromwell of Wingfield, Lord Furnival of Sheffield,
> The thrice-victorious Lord of Falconbridge;
> Knight of the noble order of Saint George,
> Worthy Saint Michael and the Golden Fleece;
> Great marshal to Henry the Sixth
> Of all his wars within the realm of France?

Pucelle replies:

> Here is a silly stately style indeed!
> The Turk, that two and fifty kingdoms hath,

> Writes not so tedious a style as this.
> Him that thou magnifi'st with all these titles
> Stinking and fly-blown lies here at our feet.
>
> (IV, vii, 60–76)

It is a theatrical coup, a *bouleversement* of the ceremonial style upheld and represented by the English "hero". That was illusion; this, says Pucelle, is the reality. So early in Shakespeare's career does the dramatist show his hand and characteristic method. But the demolition is even more complete than it looks. Pucelle's reply is addressed to Lucy, who is the latest in the series of choric messengers to chide the English nobles for their shortcomings. In IV, iv he brings Somerset the news of Talbot's fall, and laments the "private discord" that has prevented cooperation between the English forces. It is a repetition of the homily delivered by the Messenger in I, i, 71 "That here you maintain several factions". Lucy, then, faithfully maintains the choric party line. Surely, choruses are not mocked? Surely a chorus reveals at least a main strand in the playwright's argument? Then, if not earlier, we realize that Shakespeare is *not* standing behind the multiple chorus. Their line, a collective wringing of hands, is that if the English would only pull themselves together and stop quarrelling they might yet hold on to France. Which, naturally, is fair enough, up to a point, but leaves untouched the deeper causes of the English ruin. Shakespeare indicates, through Pucelle, that their obsession with the ceremonial style reveals an inner myopia; and that is the true source of their downfall.[5] Thereafter Shakespeare hastens to cover his tracks, and the black humour of Pucelle's multiple-paternity-order scene (V, iv) is her final impression on the audience. But she, and the Countess, have incarnated the Intelligence that orders this chronicle.

Richard III has four speaking parts for women: the three Queens—Margaret, Elizabeth, Anne—and the Duchess of York, Richard's mother. They constitute a single dramatic unit, though not a team comparable to the Princess of France's retinue. This unit is the chorus. The women are the element of continuity in the Civil Wars: they suffer, but survive—as no man does. They are, if you like, the faded reminder of the world of ceremony that was the England of *I Henry VI;* even Richard finds it useful to maintain the fiction of public reverence:

> Madam, my mother, I do cry you mercy;
> I did not see your grace : humbly on my knee
> I crave your blessing.
>
> (ii, ii, 104–6)

Whatever happens to their menfolk, the women remain to furnish alliances, to breed, to embellish palaces. Their expressive action is generally limited to anathema, lamentation, and foreboding, to explaining what it is like to be married to Richard or mother to politically dangerous children. They, much more than the (almost) silent citizenry, are the England of *Richard III*. They are the race memory of the nation; they are what the play *knows*.

And this cognitive function is the true role of the Intelligence in *Richard III*. The women are memory, and perception. It all leads to the remarkable episode in iv, iv, when Queen Elizabeth becomes the Prosecutor who translates Richard's conscience into words. The scene is much underrated by critics who find it a rather tedious inversion of the wooing scene. In fact, it is the necessary preparation for the Bosworth soliloquy in which Richard's conscience finds, at last, open expression; and it varies the technique of i, iv, in which the murderers become conscience and judge to Clarence. Queen Elizabeth has shown from the beginning (i, iii, 13) that she is not deceived by Richard. Here, she takes on the manner of the philosophy don, which we noted as a feature of *Love's Labour's Lost*. Extended quotation is unnecessary, but the brilliant stichomythia of iv, iv, 366–77 is typical : and this :

K. Rich.   Now, by my George, my Garter, and my crown—
Q. Eliz.   Profan'd, dishonour'd, and the third usurp'd.
K. Rich.   I swear—
Q. Eliz.   By nothing; for this is no oath :
Thy George, profan'd, hath lost his lordly honour;
Thy Garter, blemish'd, pawn'd his knightly virtue;
Thy crown, usurp'd, disgrac'd his kingly glory.
If something thou wouldst swear to be believ'd,
Swear then by something that thou hast not wrong'd.
K. Rich.   Then, by myself—
Q. Eliz.   Thyself is self-misus'd.
K. Rich.   Now, by the world—
Q. Eliz.   'Tis full of thy foul wrongs.
K. Rich.   My father's death—

Q. Eliz.   Thy life hath it dishonour'd.
K. Rich.   Why then, by God—
Q. Eliz.   God's wrong is most of all.

(iv, iv, 366–77)

It is a total refutation of the moral imbecility announced by Richard in the play's opening lines, "I am determined to prove a villain". More than that, the scene is a reversal of his particular folly. Richard's grand conceit was the perception of self as a triumphant actor. And now the Star has become the straight man : the woman, foil in the earlier wooing scene, has taken over the Star role.[6]

With *Richard III* and with *I Henry VI* we detect, at strategic points, the women expressing the consciousness of the play. The dramatic mechanism supplies variations on the technique centrally discernible in *Love's Labour's Lost*. After these experiments, matters become less clear-cut; and the technique is not obviously suited to a dramatic enterprise in which women form part of the central subject-matter of the drama. There is, however, one play of Shakespeare's maturity in which, as it seems to me, the earlier method is revived, refined, and given final expression : *King Lear*.

The opening scene gives us the geometry of relationships in the piece; they all radiate from Lear. He is bent on an act of public and private theatre, the ordering and rewarding of the major radial relationships. It is a quasi-masque, the monodrama of the beneficent Monarch. In essence, it is a deeply repellent spectacle : an old man making his will, and determined to extract the last milligramme of satisfaction as his daughters jump through the hoop for the last time. To arrive at an exact assessment of those relationships we need, I think, to investigate the "You/thou" usage, than which few notations on the linguistic score are given less attention today. A glance at the theory is worth the detour.

I take the authoritative statement to be Randolph Quirk's, and he phrases it thus :

It is often said that the old singular and plural are used in Shakespeare as they are used in Chaucer : and this is quite untrue; it is often said that in 1600 *you* was polite, formal usage but *thou* was familiar or insulting. This is a gross oversimplification : cf. McIntosh, Mulholland. The modern linguistic concept of contrast operating though *marked* and *unmarked* members can give us a truer picture. *You* is usually the stylistically un-marked form : it is not so much "polite" as "not impolite"; it is not so much "formal" as "not informal." It is for this reason that *thou* can operate in such a wide variety of contrasts with it.[7]

"Thou/you" is not an index of permanent categories, a statement of relationships always frozen into one or other form. It is a sign of living change, of mood and contrast, as people measure the degree of intimacy or distance from each other by the election of *thou* or *you*. Now Quirk uses the opening of *King Lear* as his main illustration :

> Kent, Gloucester, Edmund and Lear all use *you* in speaking to each other; as we should expect. Goneril, Regan, and Cordelia address their father as *you*—again, as we should expect. Lear addresses Goneril and Regan as *thou,* and again—from father to daughter—this is what we should expect. Against this background of perfect decorum and the fully expected, it should no doubt come as a surprise to us that Lear addresses Cordelia at first as *you* : 'what can you say to draw / A third more opulent than your sisters?' (i, i, 84 f.). So also 93 f. It seems unlikely that these uses of *you*(r) are without significance in indicating a special feeling that Lear has for the girl he calls 'our joy,' who has been, as France says, Lear's best object, the argument of his praise, the balm of his age, the best, the dearest (*ibid.* 214–16). When, however, he is shocked by what he takes to be her lack of love, he uses *thou*—not now the *thou* of father to daughter, but the *thou* of anger : 'But goes thy heart with this?' 'Thy truth, then, be thy dower!' (104, 107). This is what is meant by saying the importance lies in *active contrast*.[8]

I draw a different conclusion from Professor Quirk concerning the force of *thou* in the all-important opening exchanges. The evidence does admit of another construction. It is true, as he says, that Lear addresses Goneril and Regan as *thou*; but only *after* they have undergone the ritual of gratitude. ("We make thee lady . . . To thee and thine hereditary ever . . ." 67, 81.) The singular pronominal form does not occur before. We have the address to the three daughters ("Tell me, my daughters . . . Which of you shall we say doth love us most?"), and the separate addresses to Goneril and Regan are brief commands to "speak". Cordelia is alone in encountering the more elaborate preamble, and this contains the singular "you", "What can you say. . . ." As I read it, the address to Cordelia, taken in conjunction with the previous addresses to Goneril and Regan, supplies a clear diagram of Lear's system. His daughters are *you* before submission; *thou* after. The *you* is provisional, a not-closing of a partially open state; the *thou* is final, a grunt of satisfaction at compliance.

All this is a revelation of folly, since the realities of love and intimacy do not correspond with this crude objectification. But the folly now becomes an absurdity, and it is Cordelia's function to point it out. He asks, "what can you say to draw / A third more opulent than your sisters?" (87–8).

Before we consider the reply, let us consider the question and its background. Kent and Gloucester have already let it be known that the division is fixed, and so far as Albany and Cornwall are concerned it is finely balanced, "for equalities are so weighed, that curiosity in neither can make choice of either's moiety" (5–7). We are not told how Cordelia's portion rates against the others; but it its comparable, since Regan receives an "ample third" (82), and a third plus a third leaves a third. But that is not what Lear's words convey. "Which of you shall we say doth love us most?" is followed by "That we our largest bounty may extend / Where nature doth with merit challenge" (52–4). How can this be done? If Goneril's portion is fixed, how can the others be variable? If she is outbid by her younger sisters, how can her third be retroactively diminished? Conversely, how can the later speakers increase by the excellence of their performances the size of their portions? Lear's stated wishes, therefore, are not merely the stigmata of a domestic tyrant. They are a logical absurdity that a child could detect: a silliness.

It comes down, then, to the trigger-question that touches off the tragic action: "what can you say to draw / A third more opulent than your sisters? Speak" (87–8). What does it mean? "Draw" first: of the eleven senses Onions distinguishes, he assigns to the line the dual possibility, "to receive (money), to win a stake".[9] "Receive" seems a little innocent here: the sense of *drawing* a prize seems a stronger implication. Can we, then, infer a subdued metaphor which identifies the whole transaction as a lottery or game? Or does *draw* revert to its primary idea of "pulling", of bringing something to oneself against some kind of resistance? No aspect of these metaphoric impulses bears examination, in human terms. Then, "a third more opulent". We can just, I think, defend the phrase as containing a notion that is not absurd. It could mean "a territorial third of the kingdom, which however is richer in resources, possesses more fertile land, than the other two thirds". But the major drift (and this is certainly in line with Lear's earlier announcement of 49–54) is, what can you say to get a better portion than your sisters?

And the answer is, nothing. If the predetermined third is of a higher quality than the other two-thirds, saying will not change it. If the implication is of territorial extent, saying can only change it at the expense of the other two, whose portions are already publicly fixed. When, therefore, Cordelia breaks silence with *Nothing,* she voices the impulse of severest logic. Of course there are many emotions latent in that *nothing,* and the actress can comprehend them all. The word expresses Cordelia's mounting irritation at the performances of Lear, Goneril, and Regan, and a desire to separate herself from her appalling family. It is an impulse to punish the old man, to spoil his show. It is a reminder to him that he is making a fool of himself. It is a simple loss of temper. It is even, if you like, a failure of the intelligence, since it leads to consequences that the most righteous of daughters would not will. But if it is humanly unintelligent, it is the Intelligence of the drama that speaks. *Nothing* is the most truthful statement in the play; and it falls to a female character to announce, and to reiterate, the iron logic of the commentary.

That is the argument: Folly exposed and rebuked by Intelligence. Naturally, the agent of Intelligence has to pay her price. But Lear and Cordelia make their own accommodation, and in their final dialogue Lear freely bestows on her the "thou" of love and intimacy, "When thou dost ask me blessing . . ." (v, iii, 10).[10] It is not necessary for me to labour the structural connection of Cordelia with the Fool. *King Lear* is the agony of a single consciousness, spread across five acts; and two people, above all others, impinge upon that consciousness. It is Cordelia who says *nothing,* and the Fool who instructs Lear that "nothing can be made out of nothing" (i, iv, 145–6). We could think of the dramatic process not as a change of "perspective" (that rather bland, neutral, point-of-view term) but as "triangulation", the infantryman's metaphor for identifying a target. The consciousness at the centre of the drama is made aware of itself and its folly through two defining agents.

And my poor fool is hang'd. At last, we are in a position to read a famous crux. My readers will be familiar with the pages of notes that the Variorum lavishes upon *fool*. We know that *fool* does not identify literally the Fool, that it is a term of endearment, that it refers primarily to Cordelia. It is possible that the same actor doubled the parts of Cordelia and the Fool, and thus physically conflated the possibilities in the word. And Juliet Dusinberre is surely right in saying that "His Fool and his daughter share the same area of his consciousness."[11] But all this, in my view, skirts round the status of *fool*. Its primary force is of metaphor. "My poor fool" is Cordelia, i.e., she who had acted as Fool in challenging the imbecilities of authority. It is the terminal statement, refined to a single word, of a major resource in Shakespeare's stagecraft. Woman, the teller of truth, fuses with the Fool as representative of the Intelligence : in drama, understood.

3 *Hamlet:* Nationhood and Identity

"What *is* my nation?" wondered the Irishman, Captain Macmorris, before the walls of Harfleur; and *Henry V* is among other things the story of national identity, the fusing of English, Irish, Scots, and Welsh into British. To this theme is assimilated the personal identity of the English (or Anglo-Welsh) leader, Henry. *Henry V* is dated with certainty to 1599, a year or so before *Hamlet*. The later play takes much further the sketch of nationhood and identity presented in *Henry V*. What had been a set of literals, the overt presence of four peoples, takes on in *Hamlet* a largely metaphorical status. Everything in *Hamlet*, whatever its physical reality, is in the end subsumed into Hamlet. Events have meaning as they bear upon the consciousness at the centre of the play. And for Hamlet, the drama of his consciousness unfolds through areas of national definition. The geography of Europe becomes, in the end, countries of the mind.

This geography is distinguished by the concentration and certitude of its range. *Hamlet* is, if not a Nordic, most certainly a Northern play. Nothing in it is exotic or oriental, virtually nothing is even Mediterranean. The mousetrap play "is the image of a murder done in Vienna" (III, ii, 248), the victim is called Gonzago, and the play "written in very choice Italian" (III, ii, 273–4). The remoteness of place and language serves the immediate needs of discretion. Otherwise, there are a few references to classical Rome. Claudius is guarded (incompetently) by "Switzers" (IV, v, 97). And that is the sum of the marginalia. Everything else is focused upon six countries: Denmark, Norway, Poland, Germany, England, France. It is a Northern cluster, and even France consists here only of Normandy and Paris. They appear as real options on the play's literal (and Hamlet's mental) landscape. "*Hamlet* . . . seems to be limited to the single place of Elsinore, but much of the effect of the play comes from the desperate effort of hero and play to fulfill the standard pattern, to break out of the first place and to reach the second place".[1] But the play remains obstinately rooted in Elsinore, and the radial impulses of Hamlet, to and from the circumference, end in himself alone. Geography becomes identity.

I wish here to trace the meaning of the six major nations in *Hamlet*. They hold different significances. France implies a cultural model: Germany a role, and an escape: Norway a mirror analogue: Poland a course of action. Denmark and England hold the deepest meanings for nationhood and identity, and these countries must begin and end our enquiry.

I   DENMARK

Hamlet is a Dane. His consciousness is rooted in the collective of a single nation state. But that does not impart a security of identity to Hamlet. *Dane, Denmark* offer a primary quibble of meaning, one that Shakespeare had exploited as early as *King John*. (" 'Tis France, for England.' 'England, for itself' ", II, i, 202).[2] *Dane* is a native of Denmark, or its King. *Denmark* is the realm, or synecdoche for king. And here is part, at least, of the source of Hamlet's intense mental turbulence during I, ii, for the two words are played on repeatedly. "You cannot speak of reason to the Dane, / And lose your voice" says Claudius to Laertes (I, ii, 44–5): Hamlet, son of the late Dane, has lost his. "The head is not more native to the heart, / The hand more instrumental to the mouth, / Than is the throne of Denmark to thy father" (47–9) refers to Laertes and Polonius, and can have only the most discordant of resonances for Hamlet. Then comes the key quibble, Gertrude's "And let thine eye look like a friend on Denmark" (69). The Queen's tactic is to convey a reproach via an ambiguity. The apparent meaning is "Don't be so eager to leave your own country"; the covert rebuke is "don't look with such hostility at the King". Gertrude states the problem: Denmark is Denmark, King and country are one. And Claudius compounds the problem, with a *bêtise* presented as a courtesy: "Be as ourself in Denmark" (122). The gesture refutes itself, since it is impossible for Hamlet to be *Dane* (King) in Denmark. To the central injury Claudius adds intolerable irritation, for his satisfaction at Hamlet's capitulation speaks in "No jocund health that Denmark drinks today, / But the great cannon to the clouds shall tell, / And the king's rouse the heaven shall bruit again" (125–7). Hamlet detests the Danish reputation for hard drinking,[3] as he makes clear later; here is the King illustrating the national trait. (Hamlet ends the play refusing a drink for himself, and forcing a drink down Claudius's throat.) In sum, Claudius has taken over more than the throne, he has claimed as *Dane* a part of Hamlet's self-hood, his identity. The linguistic pointers coded in *Denmark* account for much of the acute mental disturbance in Hamlet's first soliloquy, a disturbance by no means so unequivocally founded in the actual words of the soliloquy as so many commentators assume.

The matter is elaborated in I, iv. The royal trumpet and ordnance touch off in Hamlet an acid commentary on Claudius's habits:

Hamlet   The king doth wake tonight and takes his rouse,
        Keeps wassail, and the swagg'ring up-spring reels;
        And, as he drains his draughts of Rhenish down,
        The kettle-drum and trumpet thus bray out
        The triumph of his pledge.
Horatio   Is it a custom?
Hamlet   Ay, marry, is't:
        But to my mind, though I am native here
        And to the manner born, it is a custom
        More honour'd in the breach than the observance.
        This heavy-headed revel east and west
        Makes us traduc'd and tax'd of other nations:
        They clepe us drunkards, and with swinish phrase
        Soil our addition:

                                        (I, iv, 8–20)

This is a cosmopolitan's distaste at a provincialism for which his country is notorious. It is the only passage in which Hamlet shows a concern for his country's name; the equation "my country" and "my King" is deeply irksome. The interplay of general and personal continues in the words that follow, "So, oft it chances in particular men . . ." These psychic movements solidify into the apparition of the Ghost, and Hamlet's invocation:

                        I'll call thee Hamlet,
            King, father, royal Dane:
                                        (I, iv, 44–5)

That is the statement of recognition : Hamlet, king, father, royal Dane. It is the business of the play to confirm the force of the Ghost's imperative, and for Hamlet to act on it. In acknowledging the imperative, Hamlet must affirm himself. One cannot over-emphasize the alignment of forces here : name, father, king, country. The values of patriarchy are linked with national identity; and moreover the problem, as posed, can only be resolved by an equivalence of alignment. Not until Hamlet has accepted the full implications of the alignment can he carry out his father's charge. The play's end is the affirmation of Hamlet, king, son, royal Dane.[4]

The immediate implications of the Ghost's account are symbolist. The poisoning of the king corrupts the realm, both "the whole ear of Denmark" (I, v, 36) and "the royal bed of Denmark (I, v, 82) : hence the imagistic explanation of "something is rotten in the state of Denmark" (I, iv, 90).[5] That is the position, and its elements are spelled out in Hamlet's dialogue with Rosencrantz and Guilden-stern. "Denmark's a prison . . . A goodly one, in which there are many confines, wards, and dungeons; Denmark being one of the worst" (II, ii, 247–50). There is now no possibility of resolving the contradictions in *Denmark*. "Ambition", the key word that Rosen-crantz and Guildenstern press on Hamlet, is no answer, for the excellent reason that ambition, in this context, is treason. From this impasse the Players offer some relief, and it is the more interesting if we take them to be English. Hamlet's "when I was in the city" (II, ii, 338) adds teasingly to the web of topical allusion hereabouts. It is the beginning, light and allusive, to the play's symbolic answer to the Danish problems : England.

The halted sweep to England is the movement of III, i, 177 ("He shall with speed to England") to v, i, and Hamlet's account of his travels. For Claudius, as for Hamlet, England appears as the solu-tion. For the one it is escape from prison; for the other, "cure", the chance to assert royal power ("the Danish sword", IV, iii, 63) and eliminate a problem. "Do it, England . . ." (67). Both are dis-appointed. The integrity of *Denmark* is symbolically violated by Fortinbras's march :

> *Fortinbras*   Go, captain, from me greet the Danish king :
> Tell him that, by his license, Fortinbras
> Craves the conveyance of a promis'd march
> over his kingdom.
>
> (IV, iv, 1–4)

Moreover, the claims of Claudius to be Denmark are more seriously challenged by his own people, Laertes' mob: hence the importance of Gertrude's "You false Danish dogs!" (IV, v, 110). And Hamlet is once more cast upon the shores of his prison, "naked", as Northrop Frye says, "like so many heroes of folktales".[6] He is reborn after the sea change; and his purpose is now to claim his inheritance.

It is the earth of Denmark that waits for Hamlet, and he greets it in the Gravedigger's scene "here in Denmark" (v, i, 176). The occasion is a reminder of "our last king Hamlet" (156) and his great feat of arms over Fortinbras on the day Hamlet was born. The provocations of Laertes trigger off the assertion of self in Hamlet, and it is in, not merely on, the Danish earth that he cries "This is I, / Hamlet the Dane" (280–1).[7] As Dover Wilson says, "It is noteworthy that at this first announcement to the Court of his return from England Hamlet assumes the royal title; cf. 'liegemen to the Dane'."[8] The return to Denmark has solidified in Hamlet his sense of his inheritance. As everybody notes, the change of tone is marked in Act v. This is especially clear in the v, ii dialogue with Horatio, with its recapitulation of recent events. The great underlying fact is Hamlet's acceptance of his father's mode, as politician, fighter, claimant to the throne, and ultimately ruler. The man of action is confirmed in the resourceful dispatch of Rosencrantz and Guildenstern, in the excellent pastiche of Claudius's letter-writing style, above all in the symbolism of the seal. "I had my father's signet in my purse, / Which was the model of that Danish seal" (v, ii, 49–50). Psychologically, at least, the contradictions of Denmark have disappeared for Hamlet. Elsinore is no longer a prison, but a duelling ground, as "the pass and fell incensed points / Of mighty opposites" indicates (61–2). Hamlet now prepares to claim his own.

The final scene brings together all the nations with which this play is concerned, save only Germany, forgotten since I, ii. France and Poland, Norway and England, all bear upon the final position. For the moment, only Denmark concerns us. The point to which everything leads is that Hamlet becomes, for a few minutes, the Danish King. The challenge he must overcome is Claudius's, and the King phrases it provocatively:

> The king shall drink to Hamlet's better breath;
> And in the cup an union shall he throw,

> Richer than that which four successive kings
> In Denmark's crown have worn.
>
> (v, ii, 282–5)

The occupant of the throne *drinks*, that most personally offensive of gestures, to the dispossessed, while recalling Hamlet's royal heritage. They understand one another, and Hamlet meets the challenge. In killing the King's agent, and forcing his confession, Hamlet at last faces Claudius on equal terms. The encounter is exquisitely satisfying. First, the sword-thrust, tempered with the "venom" that cures the Danish corruption. Then the spasm of appalling physical violence, repressed all through the play, with which Hamlet forces the goblet down Claudius's throat: the controlled precision of the thrust pairs with the animal ferocity of the gesture. Simultaneously the words state Hamlet's claim, and his answer to Claudius's challenge: "Here, thou incestuous, murd'rous, damned Dane, / Drink off this potion. Is thy union here?" (v, ii, 336–7). "Dane" cannot, I think, have the banal meaning "a native of Denmark" here. "Dane" is "King", and "thou", with its brutal intimacy and contempt, rightly precedes the indictment. A moment later Claudius is dead. Hamlet remains, the Dane.

His kingship does not rest upon the killing of Claudius, though it has to include that fact. It is a matter of public acceptance. The Court has done nothing to impede Hamlet in his regicide, apart from cries of "Treason!" And it could, for the killing of Claudius takes a second or two. Shakespeare has arranged matters so that Claudius does not die immediately ("Help me, friends, I am but hurt"), and this can only mean that the courtiers (and perhaps the guard) fail to come to the King's help.[9] No one on stage disputes Hamlet's total control in the final minutes of his life. The Court, which had once chosen Claudius over Hamlet, silently ratifies its election of Hamlet.[10] Hamlet himself, giving his "dying voice" in the election of Fortinbras, accepts and participates in the continuity of Danish government. So the issue to which Hamlet's last words enjoin Horatio is not simply "reputation", "name": it is legitimacy. He has become Hamlet *the Dane*, a claim he had made, with premonitory accuracy, by the graveside.

Fortinbras appears to assent: his lines contain however a trifle more reserve than is usually imputed to them. "For he was likely, had he been put on, / To have prov'd most royal . . ." (v, ii, 408–9). Shakespeare's mind, as Maynard Mack observes, seems to have been worrying at "put on" throughout the play.[11] The main associations are of disguise, costume, role. Hamlet had begun the play by dissociating himself from "actions that a man might play" (I, ii, 84); Fortinbras, at the end, hints that even the Danish King-ship did not denote him truly. Besides, Fortinbras will have his own reasons for taking a different view of the Danish succession question. Hamlet, as Fortinbras sees it, acted "like a soldier" (v, ii, 407); best pay tribute to Hamlet's version of the Polish campaign. Already Hamlet the Dane is under review.

II   NORWAY

The play ends with the Danish question arbitrated by a Norwegian. And this is fitting, for the play opens with Denmark preparing itself for a Norwegian invasion. In essence, Norway is a mirror-analogue to Denmark, and Fortinbras is a mirror-analogue to Hamlet. The comparison is plain and open. Norway is an immediate neighbour and direct challenge to Denmark. Its customs and culture are similar, if not identical. In the play even its political process is similar, for in both countries the late king is succeeded by his brother. It is the sameness, and not the differentness of Norway and Denmark that is striking. They are separate entities only in the way that North Carolina and South Carolina are separate. Norway and Denmark exist as if twinned in a controlled experiment, graded for similarities, so that the interest lies in the divergence. They do indeed diverge, but in a matched and explicit way. Fortinbras, as every commentator notes, is what Hamlet is not. I should not, myself, accept that Fortinbras is proposed by the play as a model. He is simply a personal yardstick against which Hamlet comes to measure his own conduct. Without going to the lengths of Avi Erlich—"these patronymic sons are, in many ways, equally alienated from reality, both trying to gain, in impossible ways, their father's lost power"[12]—one can agree that Fortinbras's conduct will not stand up well to close examination. It does, however, have the effect of collaborating with Hamlet's to bring about the resolution. It takes two to bring about a collaboration: no Hamlet, no successful Fortinbras.

Because of this "matched" quality of the Norway–Denmark connection, much of the necessary commentary on Norway can be supplied by repeating the Danish themes. Into "Norway" is coded the patriarchal value system, too, that of Fortinbras, King, son, royal Norwegian. All this is contained within Fortinbras's :

> I have some rights of memory in this kingdom,
> Which now to claim my vantage doth invite me.
>
> (v, ii, 400–1)

In assenting to Fortinbras, Hamlet's "dying voice" ratifies himself. For "Norway" had from the first been linked with "ambition" : "When he the ambitious Norway combated" (i, i, 61). The course of the play shows the rising tide of that same ambition in Hamlet, something he had denied to Rosencrantz and Guildenstern, recognized admiringly in Fortinbras ("divine ambition," iv, iv, 49), and confessed to Horatio ("Popp'd in between th'election and my hopes", v, ii, 65). The final position in Hamlet's life is a realization of those hopes, and the keeping of faith with his dead father. He cannot blame Fortinbras for achieving precisely this. So the triumph of the Norwegian resolves a part, a substantial part, of the Danish identity.

III   GERMANY

But these matters of patriarchy and filial obligation, of realm and politics, concern a part only of that identity. A zone of the mind's geography is elsewhere. And in *Hamlet,* the most waywardly fleeting of these countries of the mind is Germany. We know of it in one scene only, i, ii, with its four references to Wittenberg. After that it is forgotten, the land of lost content which Hamlet tries for a space to revisit, then abandons for ever. What is Wittenberg?

It is not linked with any general German characteristics. It is a university only. We know that it was famous: Luther was a student, Faustus a doctor there. "The flowering pride of Wittenberg" of which Faustus speaks (i, 113)[13] seems apt, and Fynes Moryson treated it at length in his coverage of German universities "where by the quallity of the rest may be gathered".[14] Two associations seem pre-eminent, those of its theological reputation and the literary myth. On the first count, Dover Wilson thought that :

> Hamlet, the student of Witttenberg, is chiefly swayed by Protestant prepossessions. When he first hears of the Ghost he says :

> If *it* assume my noble father's person,
> I'll speak to it though hell itself should gape
> And bid me hold my peace;

and when the apparition is before his eyes, the opening words of his speech—

> Angels and ministers of grace defend us !
> Be thou a spirit of health or goblin damned,
> Bring with thee airs from heaven, or blasts from hell,
> Be thy intents wicked or charitable

voice the orthodox Protestant standpoint.[15]

On the second, Hamlet is perhaps the inversion of Faustus. The spokesman for the mind's autonomy, for the power of the individual will, yields to the consciousness which "could be bounded in a nutshell and count myself king of infinite space, were it not that I have bad dreams".

These are possible echoes evoked by "Wittenberg". But in the play it is a very limited allusion. Hamlet in fact never even says that he wishes to return there. The King broaches the subject with a prohibition: "For your intent / In going back to school in Wittenberg, / It is most retrograde to our desire" (i, ii, 112–14), to which Gertrude adds "go not to Wittenberg" (119). When Horatio turns up, Hamlet questions him in terms that suggest less an interest in Wittenberg than a curiosity about his presence in Denmark. "And what make you from Wittenberg, Horatio? . . . But what, in faith, make you from Wittenberg? . . . But what is your affair in Elsinore?" (164, 168, 174). And that is all. In i, ii, Wittenberg is a balancing element in the diagram of psychic forces. It is easily expressed, thus:

France

↑

Denmark : Norway

↓

Witttenberg

Denmark rebuts Norway, Laertes escapes to France, Hamlet is held prisoner in Denmark. Viewed thus, Wittenberg appears less a goal in itself than a symbol of liberation. It is also regressive. Wittenberg is the past, perhaps the distant past. Bradley's argument that Hamlet was not in Wittenberg at the time of his father's death is very strong;[16] and it is easy to read an unintended implication in Claudius's "In going back to school". The phrasing leaves the interval between departure and return an open question. On the whole, I think it best to read "Wittenberg" here as a symbol of escape, rather than a positive objective.

Naturally, the university background is apt for Hamlet's cast of mind, reflective, sceptical, enquiring. It accords with Ophelia's tribute to "The courtier's, soldier's, scholar's, eye, tongue, sword" (III, i, 159), and Hamlet's welcome of Horatio as "fellow-student" (I, ii, 177). There are scattered hints of Hamlet's scholarly propensities.[17] Nevertheless, one can overstate the "scholar" aspect of Hamlet, and "Wittenberg" raises questions that will not be stilled. It is a matter of role. One who goes to a university *is* a scholar. It is an acceptance of definition. But Hamlet cannot be so defined. Consider the very phrase that appears to assert the definition beyond quibble: "The courtier's, soldier's, scholar's, eye, tongue, sword." The adjuncts—eye, tongue, sword—are not matched in parallel with the subjects. We should expect the line to conclude "tongue, sword, eye". To set the line down to a dozy printer is of course the worst treason to Shakespeare. There are more puzzles here, for does not the scholar need a tongue, and the courtier an eye? Do not courtier and scholar, like the soldier, have need on occasion of the sword? The dislocated ordering of role and adjunct is a microcosm of the play. The line is a figure of multiple identity, and the concurrent problems of definition.

I think, then, that Alexander overestimates the attractions of Wittenberg for Hamlet, and oversimplifies its function in the play:

This taken with what we see of him for ourselves satisfies us that he is a scholar, so that when father and son meet in the closing scenes of the act, not merely two types, but two ages confront one another. Wittenberg—the University—is face to face with the heroic past. From this opposition are generated the two conflicting emotions that constitute the idea that informs the play.[18]

Wittenberg, for all its attractions as a focus of role, an abandonment of responsibility, and a route of escape, can make a partial contribution only to Hamlet's identity. Moreover, location is bound up with choice. Residence in Wittenberg excludes all alternatives. Germany is not France.

IV   FRANCE

The alternative to Germany is France, as the alternative to Wittenberg is Paris. The dialectic is explicit in I, ii, when Laertes obtains leave to go, and is implied thereafter. Into the opposition of places is coded a set of values. Wittenberg is above all a monument to the intellect. Paris is the great world. It offers the most dazzling of cultural models. On this, Polonius and his son agree. For Laertes, "My thoughts and wishes bend again toward France" (I, ii, 55). The worldly old counsellor has no doubt that Paris offers the supreme standards for a travelled young man of the nobility; and his advice is explicit on the need to take note of French costuming:

> For the apparel oft proclaims the man,
> And they in France of the best rank and station
> Are of a most select and generous chief in that.
>
> (I, iii, 72–4)

The picture is touched in during Polonius' dialogue with Reynaldo, some rather different tones being added. "Inquire me out what Danskers are in Paris", following which Polonius puts words around his imagination:

> and there put on him
> What forgeries you please; marry, none so rank
> As may dishonour him; take heed of that;
> But, sir, such wanton, wild, and usual slips
> As are companions noted and most known
> To youth and liberty.
>
> *Reynaldo*   As gaming, my lord.
> *Polonius*   Ay, or drinking, fencing, swearing, quarrelling,
> Drabbing: you may go so far.
>
> (II, i, 19–26)

Paris seems to have had much the same reputation then as later. And something more of Polonius' attitude comes out, I suggest, in a single word: "Danskers". It is an unusual word, occurring here for the only time in the canon: "The Danish form" says Onions.[19] But the sound is suggestive of something else, a genially deprecatory attitude towards the described: "our Danish lads", one might say.

Is it reading too much into "Danskers" to see in it a hint of the hick, the provincial?

That, of course, would accord with Denmark's position in the world relative to France. And it would, by opposition and thus definition, help to establish another counter in this play's range of roles, one especially linked with France and Laertes: gentleman.

Polonius' advice to Laertes describes, as Honigmann remarks, "the Elizabethan's ideal gentleman, an ideal that has to be firmly stated because it asserts itself, in one disguise or another, in many scenes".[20] I should myself be cautious of accepting anything from Polonius as an ideal, the more so as the passage is aligned with the genre-scene depicted in Reynaldo's briefing, but there is no doubt that Polonius sketches in a recognizable social model. The word itself is struck frequently enough to alert us: there are twelve references to "gentleman" and twelve to "gentlemen", besides five to "gentle" and two to "gentry". What does it mean? In the first place, "gentleman" is not a clearly defined class term. Onions offers two definitions only, "officer of a company of soldiers" and "man of gentle birth attached to the household of a person of high rank". The term must be defined by context; and there is a wide range of usage in Shakespeare. At one end is Malvolio, clearly not of gentle birth, but of some education and holding down a responsible position: he can say, in a moment of extremity, "As I am a gentleman" (IV, ii, 88), and speak like one too, as the blank verse of his final outburst testifies. At the other end is Hamlet, a Prince of the blood, of whom Rosencrantz can answer the Queen's "Did he receive you well?" with "Most like a gentleman (III, i, 10–11). Rosencrantz is reassuring the Queen, telling her what she wants to hear; and there is a later hint in her message to Hamlet, "The Queen desires you to use some gentle entertainment to Laertes before you fall to play" (V, ii, 214–15) that she is anxious about this aspect of her son's conduct. For her, "gentleman" connotes simply polish. But my main point is that the term can be applied without lapse of decorum to a Prince. It is a wide gauge of conduct.

The generality of instances in *Hamlet* is unsurprising. "Gentlemen" is a convenient way of addressing several people: Hamlet can speak to Horatio and Marcellus "Unhand me, gentlemen" (I, iv, 84) and "Come hither, gentlemen" (I, v, 157): the term can imply detachment or community, hauteur as well as warmth ("So, gentlemen, / With all my love I do commend myself to you" (I, v, 183–4). The singular usage is more revealing. And the most striking point is that almost all the instances are of Laertes, or are associated with him. Reynaldo is instructed to speak of Laertes as a gentleman (II, i, 46, 53): Claudius flatters him as "a good child and a true gentleman" (IV, v, 148): Osric is ecstatic in his recognition of Laertes' qualities.

> Sir, here is newly come to court Laertes; believe me, an absolute gentleman, full of most excellent differences, of very soft society and great showing: indeed to speak feelingly of him, he is the card or calendar of gentry, for you shall find in him the continent of what part a gentleman would see.
>
> (v, ii, 110–16)

Hamlet returns the term to Osric, presumably with an ironic inflection: "The concernancy, sir? Why do we wrap the gentleman in our more rawer breath? . . . What imports the nomination of this gentleman?" (v, ii, 128–9, 113–14). A little later Hamlet consents this time without irony to the challenge: "let the foils be brought, the gentleman willing . . ." (v, ii, 182). And the category is formal in Hamlet's apologia before the Court:

> Give me your pardon, sir: I have done you wrong;
> But pardon't, as you are a gentleman.
>
> (v, ii, 237–8)

"Gentleman", then, is not really a free-floating category in *Hamlet*. It is Laertes' word, and it is used to indicate him. A gentleman is what Laertes is.

And what, then, in the terms of this play, gives Laertes his unique claim? It is his experience in France, above all. He, rare in this provincial Court, has acquired the genuine polish, not the Osric-type article, that comes only from residence in the capital of the great world. It is an ideal image; and it is the context for the fencing match.

> When Claudius remembers Lamord ("Here was a gentleman of Normandy", IV, vii, 83 ff.), Hamlet is similarly characterized by association: Claudius more or less equates Lamord and Laertes, one perfect gentleman voiced for by another, claims that Hamlet wished to match himself against Laertes, and thus implicitly measures Hamlet against Lamord, "the gem of all the nation".[21]

Laertes: France: Lamord: fencing: gentleman, is the alignment. And Hamlet must respond to it.

For Hamlet, Laertes is a personal yardstick, as Fortinbras is. He will be measured against it, and he wishes to measure himself against it. Hamlet at no time makes overt claim to the "gentleman" ideal. But he responds to it. Claudius's account is no doubt somewhat distorted:

> He made confession of you,
> And gave you such a masterly report
> For art and exercise in your defence
> And for your rapier most especial,
> That he cried out, 'twould be a sight indeed,
> If one could match you: the scrimers of their nation,
> He swore, had neither motion, guard, nor eye,
> If you oppos'd them. Sir, this report of his
> Did Hamlet so envenom with his envy
> That he could nothing do but wish and beg
> Your sudden coming o'er, to play with him.
>
> (IV, vii, 96–106)

Still, the audience is surely invited to receive this as an exaggeration of an essential truth, rather than a pure fiction. Why should Claudius bait this hook, if he had no reason to believe Hamlet would take it? When the time comes, Hamlet's admission to Horatio is unequivocal: "since he went into France, I have been in continual practice; I shall win at the odds" (V, ii, 220–2). The Queen's desire that Hamlet "use some *gentle* entertainment to Laertes" is at once satisfied, and Hamlet, in "But pardon't, as you are a gentleman" makes implicitly an equal claim for himself. His speech before the Court is the apotheosis of Hamlet as gentleman, the courtly ideal in the flesh. Laertes, "a very noble youth" (V, i, 247) is to be emulated—and surpassed.

The French context governs the terms of the wager devised by Claudius. Clearly, they are designed to bring Hamlet up to the mark. "Six Barbary horses: against the which he has impawned, as I take it, six French rapiers and poniards, with their assigns, as girdle, hangers, and so": (V, ii, 154–7). Hamlet's rephrasal is interesting. "But, on: six Barbary horses against six French swords, their assigns, and three liberal-conceited carriages; that's the French bet against the Danish" (167–70). The general sense is plain, a

France *v.* Denmark bout. The implications are subtler. The French bet is not necessarily, as one would casually take it, the French swords. Parallelism indicates that the French bet is the horses; the French, after all, are the experts in horsemanship. It is the Danes who bet (and prize) the French swords, with their liberal-conceited carriages. Hamlet's point, as I understand him, is it is just like the Danes to put up these expensive French toys. His "sword" (a good old Anglo-Saxon word) displaces "rapier" (French, new-fangled, affected, and Osrician. Cf. "Master Starve-lackey the rapier and dagger man", *Measure for Measure,* iv, iii, 16). Hamlet must have ambivalent feelings about the aura of France. The disdain with which he repeats Osric's phrases is marked; there is a touch here of an attitude expressed in a word for which no synonym or analogue exists in the English lexicon, "Frenchified", with its simultaneous derision and masked respect. Still, Hamlet controls those feelings. The outburst to Laertes over Ophelia's grave, afterwards regretted, is his last indiscipline. France, in the person of Laertes, must be surpassed, not rejected.

France, then, coded into "gentleman", locates an area of Hamlet's mind. The direct references to France, almost all of which are admiring,[22] underwrite the courtly ideal, which Laertes allegedly embodies and to which Hamlet subscribes. Beyond that, France/Germany is part of the rivalry, and antagonism, between Hamlet and Laertes. There are two underlying propositions: he who goes to Wittenberg is a scholar; he who goes to Paris is a gentleman. Hamlet is both—and neither. No one role defines him. But France, through swordsmanship, takes him closer to the core of the matter, the course of action. This challenge, and its resolution, is coded as Poland.

V   POLAND

It appeared by the history of Poland that the kingdome is elective and so limited as it rather seemes a Common Wealth then a kingdome, yet that the Polonians alwayes used such Constancye in publick Counsells, as not only they chuse the heyres males . . . but also reputed the kings widowes and daughters to pertaine to the Care of the State . . . so as they often imposed uppon the newe Chosen king the Condition, to marry the widow or daughter of the deceased king. . . .[23]

There is a curious underground linkage between the real Poland, as Fynes Moryson described it in the unpublished chapters of his *Itinerary*, and *Hamlet*.[24] Nothing of the elective system of Poland appears in this play. But it is possible that Shakespeare thought of Poland as an analogue to the Danish (elective) system. Poland's position in *Hamlet* is uniformly adversarial. The late King Hamlet confronted the Poles, as he did the Norwegians :

> *Horatio*   Such was the very armour he had on
> When he the ambitious Norway combated;
> So frown't he once, when, in an angry parle,
> He smote the sledded Polacks on the ice.
>
> (ɪ, i, 60–3)

This at once establishes the association of Poland with war. Later, when Fortinbras marches against Poland, the Captain has no doubt that the Poles will fight :

> *Hamlet*   Why, then, the Polack never will defend it.
> *Captain*   Yes, it is already garrison'd.
>
> (ɪv, iv, 23–4)

Poland is the warlike resistance that must be overcome : this is true for King Hamlet in the heroic past, and young Fortinbras in the present. It becomes, then, the symbol of the test, the opposition of war, for Hamlet.

This becomes clear enough by ɪv, iv, and Hamlet's last soliloquy. Before that point there is a strange mutation of the Polish challenge. The echoes of "Poland" in "Polonius" have often been noted.[25] I do not wish here to follow the psychoanalysts into the outer realms of speculation,[26] but shall concentrate on the main line of the variation. First, "Polonius" is Shakespeare's invention. In the Bad Quarto he is called "Corambis"; and in the degenerate descendant of the early *Hamlet* plays, *Der Bestrafte Brudermord,* he again appears as "Corambus". Shakespeare has therefore a specific point in assigning this name to the old counsellor. Second, "Polonius" has a closer suggestion of "Poland" to the Elizabethans, than to us. "Polonian" was freely used, both as an adjective and as the noun for a native of Poland. (Moryson uses the term throughout his descriptions.) Given, then, that "Polonius" is a conscious echo of "Poland", what conclusions can we derive?

The name, surely, is onomatopoeic. *Polonius* suggests a flaccid degeneration of the root *Pol*. It is not, so to speak, genuinely Polish, but an ersatz imitation. And this is precisely the judgment one applies to Hamlet's slaying of Polonius. It is an action, it is decisive and bloody. But it is a mere reflex, unplanned and unfocused, and it fails in whatever intent can be assigned to it. It is purely gestural. Killing an unarmed man behind an arras is not the real thing. Killing an armed opponent, face to face, is.

The great dual event of Act III, the play scene followed by the killing of Polonius, is at once climax and anticlimax.[27] Act III presents discovery, followed by action: these are Act v features, one might say, anagnorisis and resolution. Certainly the episodes are critical and irreversible. By Act v standards they fail. Claudius remains, and the problem has to be faced under more exacting conditions. So "Polonius" suggests, above all, an ineffectual gesture towards the Polish challenge.

Enter FORTINBRAS *with his Army over the stage.* The true model of the Polish solution follows immediately the interrogation of Hamlet concerning Polonius' corpse, and the news of Hamlet's dispatch to England (IV, iii). The scenic juxtaposition, with its vivid stage direction, makes its point: that was the imitation, this is the real thing. We have already gathered that Fortinbras, prevented from invading Denmark, has been given "his commission to employ these soldiers, / So levied as before, against the Polack" (II, ii, 74–5). Now the stage bears the imprint of Fortinbras's resolution, as he marches "Against some part of Poland" (IV, iv, 12). Hamlet learns that the point to be assailed is of no consequence in itself, but the Poles will fight: and in "How all occasions do inform against me" (IV, iv, 32 ff.) he draws his conclusions. In Fortinbras he acknowledges, at last, the ambition he had previously denied in himself: "Whose spirit with divine ambition puff'd" (IV, iv, 49). "Ambition", after all, is bound up with honour:

> Rightly to be great
> Is not to stir without great argument,
> But greatly to find quarrel in a straw
> When honour's at the stake.

> (IV, iv, 53–6)

The way is open for the acceptance of Fortinbras's example, and the correct version of the Polish solution: "O, from this time forth, / My thoughts be bloody, or be nothing worth!" (65–6).

So Hamlet, like Fortinbras, acquiesces in the form of the test. "Poland" becomes the metaphor for proving the values generated by "Denmark", as also by "Norway". The final stages of *Hamlet* belong to Fortinbras, "with conquest come from Poland" (v, ii, 361). He is the great stage image of military prowess who alone can appraise Hamlet's feat. Poland has turned out for Fortinbras to be a deviation, yet an essential step towards claiming his Danish rights. Hamlet, after the pseudo-solution of Polonius's death, has had to undergo his trial-by-combat. But Horatio, in his submission to the new authority, acknowledges another and stranger presence, "You from the Polack wars, and you from England" (v, ii, 387). The salutes which signal Fortinbras's arrival, and precede his tribute to Hamlet, are to "the ambassadors of England" (v, ii, 362).

VI   ENGLAND

England is destiny, knowledge, reality. It is the real world in and outside the playhouse, and its import breaks in upon *Hamlet* in growing rhythms and surges. At first its coming is muffled and allusive. The Players are surely English. They can be nothing else. It is unnecessary to document the tours of the English actors upon the Continent, an historical fact which helps to place and sustain their authenticity here. Much more important is the series of allusions beginning with Rosencrantz's "Even those you were wont to take delight in, the tragedians of the city" (II, ii, 341–2). The commentators have seized on "little eyases", "the children", "innovation", "Do the boys carry it away?" and so on with a special joy: these are Topical Allusions, the red meat of all good editors. And they miss, as I think, the point. The question should be: *why* does Shakespeare introduce a whole sequence of un-missable references to the London stage at this point? Shakespeare at the height of his powers, in the middle of a conscious tragic masterpiece, does not casually depart from his theme for the feeble pleasure of penning some jests at the expense of the Children of the Chapel. The purpose, as I see it, is to suggest but not name the nationality of the Players. Hamlet's "Do they hold the same estimation they did when I was in the city?" (349–50) refers (as "the City" very well may) to London.

Now here I part company from Bradley, who argued that the city "would seem to be Wittenberg".[28] It is true that the immediate text does not rebut the interpretation, and I think the mind can hold it for a while, more or less tenaciously, as a possibility. But "city" as "Wittenberg" collides with the sense of "city" as "London", which the bloc of references in ll. 339–79 very strongly advances. Moreover, the Wittenberg interpretation tends to make nonsense of Hamlet's enquiry, "How chances it they travel? their residence, both in reputation and profit, was better both ways" (343–4), because the mind is then led consciously to propose that there were indeed resident tragedians in Wittenberg, who were doing so well there that it was surprising for them to travel. And this, outside the fictive playworld, was simply not true. It must have been generally known that the Continent was not rich in resident companies. "Germany", says Fynes Moryson, "hath some fewe wandring Comeydians, ·more deserving pitty then praise",[29] and he tells somewhat patronizingly of the great impression produced by a mediocre English touring company playing at Frankfurt.[30] The natural interpretation for Shakespeare's audience would be to take "city" as "London". But I do not wish to oppose Bradley dogmatically here, for I do not think the text advances a right/wrong crux. Shakespeare is adept at both/and strategies. I propose that "city" is a purposeful ambiguity, one that contains "Wittenberg" and "London", and that the stronger possibility drives out the weaker. England drives out Witttenberg, as a mental fact. That is what happens in the play.

Let us take the Players, then, as a shaded truth, masked still but clearing. Criticism is agreed that Hamlet sees in them a figure of himself, perhaps most especially in:

Player King   What to ourselves in passion we propose,
The passion ending, doth the purpose lose.

(III, ii, 204–5)

and

Our wills and fates do so contrary run
That our devices still are overthrown;
Our thoughts are ours, their ends none of our own:

(III, ii, 221–3)

Most striking is Hamlet's admission to Horatio:

> Would not this, sir, and a forest of feathers—if the rest
> of my fortunes turn Turk with me—with two Provin-
> cial roses on my razed shoes, get me a fellowship in a
> cry of players, sir?

Horatio   Half a share.
Hamlet   A whole one, I.

(III, ii, 286–91)

The chain of association, all implied, is England: Players: self.

So much for the implied "England". The overt presence comes on in wave-like sequences, few then stronger. Here are the figures for the references to "England" (there are none to "English") III, i (2): III, iii (1): IV, iii (6): IV, vi (2): v, i (2): v, ii (7). The pattern is apparent: two in III, i, with two more trailing behind; a strong surge of six in IV, iii, with two and two to come; seven in the final scene, with England materializing in its Ambassador. It is an incoming tide that advances over Hamlet.

The details of the advance are organized with minute precision. First Claudius states it, "he shall with speed to England", and Polonius concurs, "To England send him" (III, i, 177, 194). Then Claudius imparts it to Rosencrantz and Guildenstern, "And he to England shall along with you" (III, iii, 4). Already England is the future, is Hamlet's destiny. Significantly, we are never shown the moment when the news is broken to Hamlet. It is something he already *knows* when he speaks of it to Gertrude. "I must to England: You know that?" (III, iv, 199). England focuses the mental contest between Claudius and Hamlet in IV, iii. Each mentions it three times, meaning different things by it:

> *Claudius*   and everything is bent
>   For England.
> *Hamlet*   For England.

(IV, iii, 47–8)

Pointing is vital here. Some modern editors, coarsely, place an exclamation after Hamlet's "For England!" (As if Hamlet would inflect "fancy that! well, now!"). F1 places a query there. I like best Q2's full stop, with its level, dangerous, "I'm not surprised" inflection. The emphasis matters, for Claudius has named it to

Hamlet, and *England* is death. Shakespeare had used the idea before : *Jerusalem,* which signified to Henry IV his approaching end (*2 Henry IV*, IV, v, 235), and *Rougemont,* "at which name I started, / Because a bard of Ireland told me once, / I should not live long after I saw Richmond" (*Richard III*, IV, ii, 108–10). Hamlet's immediate reaction is to repeat "England" with a certain bravado, moreover in prose which (defiantly) wrests the word from the status and meaning imparted to it in Claudius's verse. "But come, for England . . . Come, for England" (IV, iii, 50–1, 55). The threefold repetition of "England" gives the word a special resonance. Hamlet's manner appears to propose "England" as an escape route. Claudius, in soliloquy, reaffirms his sense of the matter :

> And, England . . .
>
>   . . . thou mayst not coldly set
> Our sovereign process; which imports at full,
> By letters congruing to that effect,
> The present death of Hamlet. Do it, England. . . .
>
>   (IV, iii, 60, 64–7)

First Sailor offers a new angle of perception. The letter he bears to Horatio "comes from the ambassador that was bound for England" (IV, vi, 9–10). That must have been Hamlet's joke, or the tale he told the pirates; there was no question of Claudius sending Hamlet as Ambassador. (Not in IV, iii, though the rank accords with Claudius's original intention of sending Hamlet "For the demand of our neglected tribute", III, i, 178.) "Ambassador" is in keeping with the insolent affectation of protocol of Hamlet's letter to Claudius, " 'High and mighty' " (IV, vii, 43). But of course the term directs us to Hamlet's unseen colleague, the English Ambassador. The Danish "Ambassador" to England, and his death, turns back, while the line of fate is rectified in "Rosencrantz and Guildenstern hold their course for England" (IV, vi, 28–9). The English Ambassador keeps his appointment in Denmark. Hamlet and England will miss each other, and yet they will meet.

The Clowns in Shakespeare invariably express matters of import, and England passes through the earthy hands of the First Gravedigger :

> it was the day that young Hamlet was born; he that
> is mad, and sent into England.

Hamlet	Ay, marry, why was he sent into England?
First Clown	Why, because 'a was mad: 'a shall recover his wits there; or, if 'a do not, 'tis no great matter there
Hamlet	Why?
First Clown	'Twill not be seen in him there; there the men are as mad as he.

(v, i, 160–70)

Birth, madness, travel, a dubious sanity, England: that is what the Clown knows about Hamlet. It is a curious passage, one which always wins a laugh in the theatre and brings the play closer to the real world, as the skull and earth bring Hamlet closer to his mortality. England seems here to stand in some undefined yet vital relationship to madness and sanity, to the reality of the outside world and the reality of death. England now takes on the shape of the truth, which is beginning to penetrate the play's consciousness.

It is a cloudy symbol, but clearing rapidly as the crisis of v, ii, approaches. In Hamlet's account to Horatio, "England" is a kind of fiction, both for Claudius and himself. "Importing Denmark's health, and England's too . . ." which becomes "As England was his faithful tributary . . ." (v, ii, 21, 39). For both, "England" is a device, a tactic. But Horatio knows, and his thoughtful:

> It must be shortly known to him from England
> What is the issue of the business there.

(v, ii, 71–2)

brings events into perspective: again, the combination of "England" and "know". But this time the implication is of ineluctable Fate. England is knowledge, and destiny, and death. Hamlet knows it too, and his response, gnomic and balanced, is his "perfect soul" as he awaits his fate:

> It will be short: the interim is mine;
> And a man's life's no more than to say 'One.'

(v, ii, 73–4)

When it comes, "What warlike noise is this?" (v, ii, 360), Hamlet receives England as a summons.

> *Osric*   Young Fortinbras, with conquest come from Poland,
>   To the ambassadors of England gives
>   This warlike volley.
>
> (v, ii, 361–3)

It signals the death-throe:

> *Hamlet*   O, I die, Horatio;
>   The potent poison quite o'ercrows my spirit:
>   I cannot live to hear the news from England . . .
>
> (v, ii, 363–5)

Hamlet's final speech is the response to the coming of the Ambassador.

England is Hamlet's appointment in Samarra. He had tried to leave Elsinore, and escape to England; now England, and his fate, and death come to him in Elsinore. The English Ambassador, like Mercade, is the messenger who comes bearing the tidings of death —"That Rosencrantz and Guildenstern are dead"—only to encounter it, surprised, "here in Denmark". As the action draws towards its close, the play-world of Elsinore merges with the daylight and reality of the English stage, and the greatest and least understood alienation effect in Shakespeare takes place:

> *First Ambassador*   The sight is dismal;
>   And our affairs from England come too late:
>   The ears are senseless that should give us
>   hearing,
>   To tell him his commandment is fulfill'd,
>   That Rosencrantz and Guildenstern are dead.
>   Where should we have our thanks?
>
> (v, ii, 378–83)

"Where should we have our thanks?" Who is responsible? *Hamlet,* which begins in darkness, ends in a kind of daylight. Horatio can "truly deliver" what he knows, but it is no more than we do. Fortinbras orders the right obsequies, but "Bear Hamlet *like* a soldier" contains the reservation that one only of the many roles, because uppermost, is apt. "*For* he was likely, had he been put on, / To have prov'd most royal" deepens the reservation. In this play of many questions, the messenger from England asks the last. The question, tabled by the Englishman, remains unanswered.

4 Hierarchic Forms: Language and Structure in *Measure for Measure*

The structure of *Measure for Measure* is expressed through a dual location system not found elsewhere in Shakespeare. It is usual for Shakespeare to oppose geographic locations, each symbolizing and generating a complex of values: thus, court and country, Egypt and Rome, Venice and Belmont. Even in plays where the dual setting scheme is less apparent, a change of milieu does hold its significances: Hamlet's abortive journey to England evidently signals a change of mental direction. All these instances involve geographic change, "travel" in its customary sense, for the protagonists. *Measure for Measure* is unique: it is set within the boundaries of a single city, Vienna,[1] yet presents an opposition between the underworld, whose control mechanism is prison, and the overworld. It is, schematically, an upstairs-downstairs play in which the structural alternations are vertical. All the conventionally identifiable scene settings—nunnery, grange, a public place, "Vienna", courtroom, prison—conform to this principle. And these settings present as dramatic realities the energies of *Measure for Measure*.

This governing idea encompasses a complete society, a community whose values are fully realized in the dramatist's selection of material. The overworld is founded on government, restraint, morality, shame, discipline; its main representatives are the Duke, Angelo, Isabella, Escalus. The underworld exists for the free gratification of impulses controlled or suppressed elsewhere; its leading citizens are Pompey and Mistress Overdone. Between these worlds is an iron grid, the law of the land. And that barrier is in effect impassable save to men about town and officers of the law. This is no organic society, no Navarre in which Costard can exchange ruderies with a lady of the court. The leading proof of the social divide is Lucio. Shaw observed of him long ago :

> Lucio is much more of a gentleman than Benedick, because he keeps his coarse sallies for coarse people. Meeting one woman, he says humbly, 'Gentle and fair : your brother kindly greets you. Not to be weary with you, he's in prison.' Meeting another, he hails her sparklingly with 'How now? which of your hips has the more profound sciatica?' The one woman is a lay sister, the other a prostitute. Benedick or Mercutio would have cracked their low jokes on the lay sister, and been held up as gentlemen of rare wit and excellent discourse for it.[2]

Shaw is technically in error here (the "sciatica" greeting is spoken by First Gentleman : doubtless Shaw's memory of a production betrayed him), but right in substance. Lucio makes a sharp distinction between the two worlds that he moves in, and his speech signals the change unmistakably. With his male friends, with Pompey, with the backstairs Friar, his language is prose. It is fluid, inventive, bawdy, malicious. With Isabella, and with the Duke in the final scene, his language is verse : decent, restrained, rather unctuous. "I hold you as a thing enskied and sainted" reflects the pedestal on which the virtuous woman is placed. Simply, Lucio distinguishes between being on his best behaviour (in the over-world) and indulging himself. The verse–prose switches of Lucio are one way of identifying the inner characteristics of Vienna; another is the role of Juliet. Her only speaking scene is ɪɪ, iii, and this is entirely superfluous to the general needs of the action. It appears therefore as an emblem-scene, whose function is to present a speaking picture of sin and shame, the pregnant Juliet. The Duke's judgment is society's "As that the sin hath brought you to this shame" (ɪɪ, iii, 31), and Juliet's submission is a perfect acceptance of the social imperative : "I do repent me, as it is an evil, / And take the shame with joy" (35–6). Evil, which in this society is conceived primarily in sexual terms, is above all detectable in pregnancy. But until then it is veiled, prohibited, surmised.

We grasp, then, a society in which vertical communication between its two main divisions is at all times difficult. The body politic appears imperfectly aware of the functioning of its separate parts. So much is apparent in a notable characteristic of Vienna's citizens, evasion or euphemism. Claudio finds it impossible to answer directly to his friend's enquiry "What's thy offence, Claudio?" (I, ii, 138–9). Lucio, after trying "murder" and "lechery", has to come out with the truth himself, in the wake of Claudio's involved explanation: "With child, perhaps?" Shame dominates Claudio,[3] and he is thankful to acquiesce in Lucio's wording of the matter: "Unhappily, even so" (160). It then becomes Lucio's problem to break the same news to Isabella, and he succumbs to the same psychological difficulties. His first attempt is indeed direct:

> For that which, if myself should be his judge,
> He should receive his punishment in thanks:
> He hath got his friend with child.
>
> (I, iv, 27–9)

But his follow-up is largely circumlocution:

> Fewness and truth, 'tis thus:
> Your brother and his lover have embrac'd;
> As those that feed grow full, as blossoming time
> That from the seedness the bare fallow brings
> To teeming foison, even so her plenteous womb
> Expresseth his full tilth and husbandry.
>
> (I, iv, 39–44)

Two points here. "Fewness and truth" is sheer window-dressing, for the unctuous tautology of the imagery is scarcely redeemed by the pun on "husbandry". These lines amplify the earlier statement but add nothing. Then, "lover": Lucio discreetly refrains from naming the guilty one. Isabella guesses Juliet anyway, and Lucio confirms the guess after a hesitation, but he would not otherwise have identified her. There is a resistance to openness in this society; it is secretive, evasive, euphemistic.[4] This is seen clearly in the caricature of its mores that the underworld supplies. The trash apes gentility, and Pompey finds it necessary to excuse a notorious allusion: "Sir, she came in great with child; and longing, saving your honour's presence, for stewed prunes . . ." (II, i, 91–2). Pompey, evidently, feels it keenly when Escalus extracts from him his unfortunate surname. I suggest, then, that language, reflecting the prevailing spirit of Vienna, imparts a distinctive concern with tabu and propriety.

It is an easy progression, then, to arrive at an estimate of the dramatic forces in *Measure for Measure*. The dual location system, allied to the observed characteristics of Viennese society, figures a dialectic of liberty and restraint, freedom and imprisonment. So much is obvious: but the dialectic is not, of course, a simple matter of debating oppositions, of Angelo versus Pompey. Rather, what emerges is a total play which presents a completely synthesized account of the dialectic. J. I. M. Stewart's excellent commentary on *Othello* is suggestive here:

> I conjecture, then, that at certain cardinal moments in the play when poetically received Othello and Iago are felt less as individuals each with his own psychological integrity than as abstractions from a single and, as it were, invisible protagonist.[5]

Similarly, the characters in *Measure for Measure* can easily be comprehended as representing inclinations on a liberty-restraint scale; but the human and dramatic truth of the characters depends upon the proposition that these contrary impulses co-exist in the same mind. Thus, we become aware that these impulses are not merely present in a single intense encounter (Isabella–Angelo) but animate the entire play, impelling or inhibiting the dramatis personae in any line they take. Claudio and Juliet are as conscious of guilt as previously eager for each other; Abhorson and Pompey have an equal taste for respectability ("he will discredit our mystery"); the contradictions of Angelo need no catalogue. *Measure for Measure* forces upon us a continuous awareness of the dialectic, until we perceive the play ultimately as *nothing else*: that is, that the apparatus of prison and overworld is simply a physical model for the mental forces that animate the play. Self-indulgence, self-repression, self-knowledge are the primary concerns of this play.

II

It is clear that we are circling around the entire question of the sexual element in *Measure for Measure*, and indeed that the restraint–freedom dialect can be discussed in terms of the Freudian mental model. We have then to appraise this sexual element. Eric Partridge, in his pioneering study, found that *"Measure for Measure* and *Othello* are Shakespeare's most sexual, most bawdy plays".[6] Reasonable as this judgment appears, it suggests a possible confusion of categories: "sexual" is not the same as "bawdy".[7] The bawdy in *Measure for Measure* comprises the linguistic territory of Pompey and Lucio, with help from Elbow. I regard it as the actualization of tendencies present elsewhere, the covert, latent sexuality that permeates the entire piece. "Sexual" I prefer to employ in its wider sense, as a description of impulses of desire and repression that tend towards, but may stop short of the threshold of, sexual congress.[8] The nature of these impulses is unremittingly probed through the action and language of *Measure for Measure*.

Nothing need be said of the plot, save that it is based to a degree not found elsewhere in the canon on the *fact* of the sexual act. The comedies are broadly concerned with love as a value associated with sexuality. So, too, is *Othello,* since the tragedy stems from a sense of betrayed love. *Measure for Measure* does not examine love, other than by inference. It rests on the state's will to interdict all extramarital congress. And from this central fact emerges a certain symbolism. First and most obvious is the matter of beheading. We have it on Freud's authority that beheading occurs frequently in dreams as a substitute for castration; it is a psychoanalytic commonplace.[9] But we scarcely need the later authority, since the play presents, in its own terms, beheading as an associate of castration. The beheading of Claudio is an explicit punishment for the sexual act. Pompey, as usual, provides the bawdy-variant of the issue: "Does your worship mean to geld and splay all the youth of the city?" (II, i, 242–3). The answer, in symbolic language, is "yes": that is exactly what the law intends. Pompey's line is the play's only explicit reference to castration, but this deep sense of the punishment's objective pervades the play. It is perhaps most effectively confirmed in Isabella's "There is a vice that most I do abhor, / And most desire should meet the blow of justice" (II, ii, 29–30).

Again, consider the symbolism of Angelo's garden-vineyard. As J. W. Lever points out, "No mention of a garden assignation appears in the sources": it is an imaginative addition by Shakespeare. Lever goes on to note that " 'garden houses' in the suburbs were associated with secret love trysts".[10] To this local association one can add the general and permanent symbolic values. Freud lists "gardens" as "common symbols of the female genitals"[11] and this accords very well with the immediate and specific associations of Angelo's trysting-place. The luxuriant, secretive garden-vineyard of Isabella's description (IV, i, 28–36), with the culminating reference to the "heavy middle of the night", generates strongly sexual overtones. These are clarified into Mariana's later claim "in's garden house, / He knew me as a wife" (v, i, 229–30). "Garden", in this play, carries suggestions that unite Freud and the historian of Elizabethan usage.

Less obvious but worth noting is the by-play with "key". Clearly (a point one has sometimes to make concerning the more enthusiastic psychoanalytic commentators) there must be occasions in literature when the object is permitted to be itself alone, sans symbolism. Agreed, but Shakespeare does impart a sense of special importance to "key" here. The Nun, hearing Lucio outside, reacts immediately :

> It is a man's voice. Gentle Isabella,
> Turn you the key, and know his business of him;
> You may, I may not; you are yet unsworn;
>
> (I, iv, 7–9)

In dramatic context the opening of a door to a man is viewed as a potentially sexual act; the key mediates the process, and to Isabella is entrusted control. Those who resist Freud's formulation (key = penis)[12] at this point may find more convincing the later episode, in which Isabella receives from Angelo the keys to his vineyard and inner garden. Since the purpose of the transaction is overtly sexual, the resonance of this line is formidable : "That makes his opening with this bigger key . . ." (IV, i, 31). Always, in *Measure for Measure,* it is the force of the action itself that imparts sexual energy to situations and allusions which (in another play) would be relatively innocent. It is, however, through the play's language that the most extensive documentation of its sexual concerns can be made.

III

The language of *Measure for Measure* reflects in diffused but fully realized form the concerns of the play. That which is repressed, that which forces itself upwards towards consciousness, that which is known : these are the elements that language, no less than dramatic structure, must convey. It is above all a matter of vocabulary. We are concerned with words that impart a hierarchy of meanings, meanings that fall easily into a higher and lower division. And this is not the same as the general multiplicity of meanings found everywhere in Shakespeare, nor is it the simple trick of double entendre that every Jacobean playwright has at his fingertips. Broadly, the language of *Measure for Measure* tends to crystallize into a lower—essentially, a sexual—implication, as well as the higher sense in which it is formally employed.

We can begin with the act of government. It is on four occasions imaged as the action of riding a horse, itself the most potent of symbols of sexual activity:[13]

> Or whether that the body public be
> A horse whereon the governor doth ride,
> Who, newly in the seat, that it may know
> He can command, lets it straight feel the spur . . .
>
> (I, ii, 163–6)

That is Claudio's account. The Duke has:

> We have strict statutes and most biting laws,
> The needful bits and curbs to headstrong jades . . .
>
> (I, ii, 19–20)

Angelo adds to the cluster with "And now I give my sensual race the rein" (II, iv, 160), and the Duke rounds it off with:

> He doth with holy abstinence subdue
> That in himself which he spurs on his pow'r
> To qualify in others.
>
> (IV, ii, 84–6)

The proposition is that government expresses a subdued sexual satisfaction for the governor, though the Duke is careful to state a rationale for his sense of the image. "Satisfaction", then, becomes a word less than fully innocent, and we notice that it is used only by Angelo and the Duke (twice each). It tends towards *OED* sense 5, "The action of gratifying (an appetite or desire) to the full . . ." and its occurrences are worth quoting in order:

Angelo (to Escalus) Let us withdraw together,
And we may soon our satisfaction have
Touching that point.

(I, i, 81–3)

Duke (to Isabella)   I would by and by have some speech with
you : the satisfaction I would require is like-
wise your own benefit.

(III, i, 155–7)

Duke (to Isabella)   . . . give him [Angelo] promise of satisfaction.

(III, i, 275)

Angelo (to Provost) For my better satisfaction let me have
Claudio's head sent me by five.

(IV, ii, 126–7)

These passages demonstrate the "hierarchic" principle of meanings
that I have proposed. (1) is innocent, since "satisfaction" means
"resolution of doubt"; (2) suggests fulfilment of (undisclosed but
legitimate) wish; (3) means sexual satisfaction; and (4) a gratification of totally illegitimate desires. The doubt which the action pro-
gressively throws on "satisfaction" surely culminates in the Duke's
injunction to Angelo, "And punish them to your *height of
pleasure*" (v, i, 240). And these meanings are strengthened by the
ambivalences of "act". Claudio, in a passage of early importance,
has :

and, for a name,
Now puts the drowsy and neglected act
Freshly on me.

(I, ii, 173–5)

The play is on the legal (government) and sexual senses. The prime
meaning, via "neglected", evidently relates the statement to the
law. But "drowsy" creates a sexual dimension, and the passage's
secondary meaning appears as "blames me for a careless ('neglected') and sleepy act". ("He hath but as offended in a dream",
as the Provost observes, II, ii, 4 : Partridge thought the phrase
especially worthy of citation as euphemistic.)[14] Shakespeare repeats
the play on "act" via Lucio: "He . . . hath pick'd out an act /
Under whose heavy sense your brother's life / Falls into forfeit . . ."

(I, iv, 62–6). "Heavy" perhaps attracts the transferred sense of "sleepy" (cf. "the heavy middle of the night", IV, ii, 25). "Act" is coloured by the near presence of "law" and "statute", yet carries the sexual possibility, to which "sense" contributes. "Act" has in *Measure for Measure* the effect of associating the action of government with the sexual impulse.

The dramatic tendency of these passages is to question the purity of the Duke's motives. And this challenge is sustained elsewhere, sharply or insidiously. We are, for instance, led towards viewing Angelo as the Duke's agent in the fullest sense. Even in the opening scene the sexual vibrations are easily detectable. "Pregnant" (line 11) is not, in this play, an innocent metaphor, and the Duke's account of his policy is striking :

> . . . we have with special soul
> Elected him our absence to supply;
> Lent him our·terror, dress'd him with our love,
> And given his deputation all the organs
> Of our own power.
>
> (I, i, 18–22)

Again, "But I do bend my speech / To one that can my part in him advertise . . ." (I, i, 41–2). It is not necessary to press the interpretation that Angelo is acting out the concealed desires of his master; it is sufficient to note the linguistic cruces that direct us to think along these lines. One of the sharpest hints occurs very late, when Angelo protests that his accusers are "But instruments of some more mightier member / That sets them on" (v, i, 237–8). *Member* has the general sense of "a part or organ of the body", but the *OED* allows special sanction to "privy member".[15] In any case the word is coloured by its one previous application, by Pompey of all people. "Your whores, sir, being *members* of my *occupation*" (IV, ii, 39), after which it might seem a scholarly reservation even to admit of an additional, higher sense. No word retains its innocence after Pompey has used it.

A curiously reversed process occurs with *motion*. We noted with "satisfaction" a progressive deterioration of moral status, from resolution of doubt to desire. Now with "motion", the final occurrence attempts to wrest it from an established meaning. The Duke, in his closing speech, has :

> Dear Isabel,
> I have a motion much imports your good . . .
>
> (v, i, 531–2)

"Motion" can only mean "proposal" here; it is clearly a sense of the utmost propriety, not unreminiscent of our modern sense of formal debate. Yet we have to recall its three previous occurrences:

> *Lucio*   one who never feels
> The wanton stings and motions of the sense . . .
>
> (i, v, 58–9)

> *Claudio*   This sensible warm motion . . .
>
> (iii, i, 120)

> *Lucio*   And he is of a motion generative . . .
>
> (iii, ii, 118–19)

The speakers define the word. For Claudio, *l'homme moyen sensuel*, it is life itself, the movement of the body and its desires. For Lucio "motion" is the lusts of the flesh. Here the history of this word suggests in microcosm Lucio's scene with the disguised Duke (iii, ii), in which the dual motives and sexual inclinations are consistently slandered. Malicious or not, Lucio's function is to set up doubts in the audience which the Duke's rebuttal cannot entirely dismiss. (Indeed, his "I never heard the Duke much *detected* for women", iii, ii, 129–30, seems a classic instance of the Freudian slip.) When, therefore, the Duke employs "motion" to describe his initiative towards Isabella, the word is already devalued.

"Know" is the easiest instance of this tendency. As all agree, *Measure for Measure* is much concerned with self-knowledge: the Duke's "Pattern in himself to know" (iii, ii, 277) and Angelo's "What art thou, Angelo?" (ii, ii, 173) suggest that for both the action is a journey into the interior of self.[16] But I want to emphasize the importance of "know" in the final scene. It is heavily stressed in the Mariana–Duke passage (eight times in 27 lines, v, i, 187–213), especially in Mariana's:

> Who thinks he knows that he ne'er knew my body,
> But knows he thinks that he knows Isabel's.
>
> (v, i, 203–4)

The point of this word play is given to Lucio to dramatize:

Duke Know you this woman?
Lucio Carnally, she says.
                    (v, i, 213–14)

A very old dual sense of "know", this: yet Shakespeare insists on the point, and wrings a laugh out of it too. He will not let the dual sense escape here; yet in *Much Ado,* a comedy of romance that exploits "know" consistently, he all but excludes the carnal sense.[17]

In fine, a central cluster of words can be shown to have tendencies towards higher and lower meanings. It is unnecessary for me to analyse at length the word which bears the weight of the entire linguistic and dramatic enterprise, *sense,* since this has been accomplished in William Empson's classic study in *The Structure of Complex Words.* "Sense" occurs on twelve occasions, with the general meaning of "reason", "decent feeling" on the one hand, and "sensuality" on the other. The representative passages are:

Lucio   The wanton stings and motions of the sense . . .
                    (i, iv, 59)

Angelo She speaks, and 'tis such sense
         That my sense breeds with it.
                    (ii, ii, 141–2)

Duke   Her madness hath the oddest frame of sense . . .
                    (v, i, 61)

Duke   Against all sense you do importune her.
                    (v, i, 438)

Though the possibilities here are much more complex than with the other terms discussed, the word exhibits the general dualism I have argued for, and I accord with Empson's conclusion: "the performance with the word *sense* is made to echo the thought of the play very fully up to the end".[18] The term verges on homograph, for "sense" must cover a wide range of mental and physical activity. In its division between sexual and rational/ sensibility meanings, it corresponds to the dual location structure and to the dialectic of freedom–restraint. "Sense", even more than the other terms we have considered, contains the genetic code of the play.

IV

Language is character, and we can move from the vital areas of the play's language to the characters who speak it. Claudio is a convenient beginning. Early in the play he says of Isabella:

> For in her youth
> There is a prone and speechless dialect
> Such as move men; beside, she hath prosperous art
> When she will play with reason and discourse,
> And well she can persuade.
>
> (I, ii, 187–91)

Lever remarks: "There is an undercurrent of irony in the equivocal words 'prone', 'move', and 'play', all capable of suggesting sexual provocation."[19] Precisely: and Lever's observation applies as cogently to the preceding "Implore her, in my voice, that she make *friends* / To the strict deputy; bid herself *assay* him." But the real point is that this passage is so entirely typical of the play; the leading characters all express themselves in this mode, with its undercurrent of sexuality. Isabella's own language combines an underlying awareness of sexuality with an overt determination on chastity. Her opening words are a commitment to self-restraint: "I speak not as desiring more, / But rather wishing a more strict restraint" (I, iv, 3–4). And her address to Angelo places the intensity of her commitment beyond question:

> There is a vice that most I do abhor
> And most desire should meet the blow of justice . . .
>
> (II, ii, 29–30)

Still, the repressed sexuality of her temperament is very clear in:

> Th'impression of keen whips I'd wear as rubies,
> And strip myself to death, as to a bed
> That longing have been sick for, ere I'd yield
> My body up to shame.
>
> (II, iv, 101–4)

Her scene with Claudio (III, i) has a strong erotic tension. The progression is interesting:

Isabella   In such a one as, you consenting to't,
             Would bark your honour from that trunk you bear,
             And leave you naked.

(III, i, 71–3)

Claudio   If I must die,
             I will encounter darkness as a bride,
             And hug it in mine arms.

(83–5)

Isabella   Is't not a kind of incest, to take life
             From thine own sister's shame?

(139–40)

The allusions intensify. "Incest", the culminating word, presents Isabella's yielding to Angelo as a symbolic congress with her brother. The psychological reality here appears as extreme revulsion, tinged with a certain awareness of the erotic charge in "incest".[20] I am not, of course, proposing a full-dress psychoanalytic interpretation of Isabella based on a supposed regard for her brother, in the manner of *The Duchess of Malfi* and *A King and No King*. One could as well pursue the implications of her exchange of names with Juliet, "By vain though apt affection" (I, iv, 48). I suggest rather that there is in her an undischarged sexual tension that reveals itself in the erotic element in her language. To the obvious instances can be added her retort to Angelo, "I would to heaven I had your potency, / And you were Isabel!" (II, ii, 67–8), for *potency* contains the same suggestion. It is true that the *OED* does not give "possessing sexual power" for "potency"; but this is a word impossible to separate completely from its fellows, *potent* and *impotent*, in the seamless web of language, and these terms undoubtedly admit the sexual implication at the time of *Measure for Measure*. It is clear, as one reviews the six instances of "potency" and twenty of "potent" in Shakespeare, that the uppermost sense is of temporal power. But *Antony and Cleopatra* has "And gives his potent regiment to a trull" (III, vi, 95), and the *OED* cites "impotency" with the sexual sense from 1594. Isabella's wish, then, expresses itself through a term already tinged with what, in the later history of the language, was to become the strong implication of male (*and* female) sexual capacity. In sum, Johnson's celebrated comment on Isabella's late flash of sexual vanity ("I partly think /

A due sincerity govern'd his deeds / Till he did look on me" (v, ii, 450–2):

> I am afraid our varlet poet intended to inculcate that women think ill of nothing that raises the credit of their beauty and are ready, however virtuous, to pardon any act which they think incited by their own charms,[21]

appears less an intrusion of eighteenth-century cynicism than a sound perception that Isabella's self-knowledge—and hence, sexual awareness—has been growing throughout the play. This speech is her last, and combined with her silence towards the Duke's overtures is the formal culmination of the state of awareness she has reached by the end of *Measure for Measure*.

Angelo's thoughts and actions are specifically directed towards the sexual act, and as such they require little commentary. Even so, it is striking that the language in which he expressed his inclination is so often veiled, allusive, suggestive. It is as though he finds difficulty in admitting the extent of his propensity, even to himself; and in this sense his language is indeed an amplification of the wondering "What *art* thou, Angelo?" For instance, "And in my heart the strong and swelling evil / Of my conception" (ii, iv, 6–7) projects the physical implications of *conceive*, while holding nominally to the mental sense. (The further, glancing possibility that *conception is evil* may help the actor.) The same physicality looms in:

> This deed *unshapes* me quite, makes me *unpregnant*
> And *dull* to all proceedings. A *deflower'd* maid!
> And by an eminent *body* that *enforc'd*
> The law against it!
>
> (iv, iv, 23–6)

The first line and a half convey a mental state, yet the impression is as much of detumescence as of depression; it is a plain case of *post coitum omne animal triste est*. Again, his first reaction to Isabella contains the lines:

> Having waste ground enough
> Shall we desire to raze the sanctuary
> And pitch our evils there?
>
> (ii, ii, 170–2)

The play is on *evil*, which means "privy" also. This repellent symbolism for the sexual act takes up, via "corrupt", the "carrion" idea in line 167 of the same soliloquy. But above all sex is a "temptation" (182), and the "hook" image with which Angelo expresses the thought;

> O cunning enemy, that, to catch a saint,
> With saints dost bait thy hook !
>
> (II, ii, 180–1)

parallels strikingly Isabella's sense of the situation :

> O perilous mouths,
> That bear in them one and the self-same tongue
> Either of condemnation or approof;
> Bidding the law make court'sy to their will,
> Hooking both right and wrong to th'appetite,
> To follow as it draws !
>
> (II, iv, 172–7)

Both Angelo and Isabella perceive each other as a dangerous adversary, as a tempter. Since it is impossible to be tempted by what one does not wish, it is the play's function to delineate the source of this profound attraction.

The Duke focuses the play; as, on standard Shakespearean form, we should expect. Shakespeare has an abiding sense of the ways in which a community is symbolized in its ruler : the fever-stricken John as emblem of England's internal war, Richard the ravening boar, the strong-willed but uncomprehending Prince of Verona. A ruler generates, reflects, and exemplifies the values of his realm. Commentators and directors have varied widely in their perception of the Duke as a semi-religious figure, God's Viceroy,[22] and as an "unctuous fraud".[23] It seems clear, as one reviews the general linguistic pattern of *Measure for Measure,* that the issue is not best stated in direct moral categories at all, as fraud versus holy man. It is a matter of the human mind coming to terms with itself. Our experience of the Duke is analogous to his speeches in the opening scene, which move from a bafflingly contorted and obscure syntax to a clear, easily flowing style. The early part is concerned with giving an account of himself, the latter with giving orders. So the movement from shadow to clarity is contained even in the opening; and we retain this sense of the Duke at the close.

Much of what has already been cited applies to the Duke, is indeed spoken by him. I select a few crucial passages to amplify the sketch of him that has emerged. The Duke, ever ready—until the final scene—to disclaim any sexual interest has an early denial: "Believe not that the dribbling dart of love / Can pierce a complete bosom" (i, iii, 2–3). (Whatever can be said of "dribbling" as "falling wide/short of the mark", the underlying phallic possibility remains.) This brief challenge and parry is amplified into the Lucio–Duke episode of iii, ii. "The Duke", as Vickers observes, "sees himself in that divine Renaissance triplicity: 'a scholar, a statesman, and a soldier' ";[24] Lucio sees an aged roué: the composite image is the play. Now nothing in the entire action vexes the Duke so much as Lucio's scandal mongering. His immediate reaction is fierce; the only real punishment he hands down at the end is to Lucio; and in an intervening scene, *à propos* of nothing at all, he launches into the following:

> O place and greatness! millions of false eyes
> Are stuck upon thee . . . thousand escapes of wit
> Make thee the father of their idle dream . . .
>
> (iv, i, 60–4)

It is a fascinating reference to the tendency of humanity to project fantasies upon the great (cf. Jonson's scurrilities to Drummond of Hawthornden on the subject of Queen Elizabeth).[25] The dramatic impression so insidiously conveyed is that there is *something* to it. Lucio's "I am a kind of burr; I shall stick" objectifies an impulse of the drama. And after all, the "complete bosom" is pierced by the final scene.

What, then, are we to make of the "pattern in himself to know" address? Its primary characteristic is an archaic form and broad allusion: it appears as an Everyman monologue as much as a soliloquy. On the principle that all speeches in mature Shakespearean drama are compatible with a naturalistic psychological explanation, I propose that we regard the soliloquy as a kind of incantation. The speech, an expanded sententia, is a *reminder* to himself of his role. The Duke is stating, for the purposes of self-rectification, the acknowledged premises on which a ruler should proceed. Even so, "weed *my vice* and let his grow" is decidedly arresting. I can see little point in a critical sanitizing of "my vice" as "Everyman's". The suggestion is obvious and immediately available in the theatre. That, if you like, is the acknowledged premise. The Duke appeals to a past tradition as the guardian of his persona.

On this approach, then, we can see the final scene as a public exorcisement by the Duke of impulses in himself. After "We do condemn thee to the very block / Where Claudio stoop'd to death" (v, i, 419–20), the Duke enacts Angelo, as Mariana and Isabella kneel to him. The key line then becomes, "I find an apt remission in myself" (503), surely a vector that indicates the Duke's share in the flawed humanity of his realm. As for the proposal to Isabella, Sachs's commentary here is suggestive:

> As Angelo's wedding parallels on a higher level the enforced marriage of Lucio, so performs the Duke, in a legitimate and honourable way, the crime which Angelo attempted in vain.[26]

Recent stage practice, we can note, has fully grasped that *Measure for Measure's* ending is not a bland churching, a slice of the higher kitsch.[27] We remain, in the text's own terms, with a marked lack of response to a truly surprising psychological dénouement. Why not accept the Duke's late conversion to marriage as the key fact of the drama, and read it backwards from there?

That concludes the analysis. I add a postscript: the play, from the same perspective, can be thought of as Barnardine's. One of the great images of *Measure for Measure* is of Barnardine, that unregenerate life force, rising up from the ground to assert his own shameless existence. I am aware that a trap-door is not essential to the staging here; and Hosley, in his survey of plays designed for original performance at the First Globe playhouse, has shown that *Measure for Measure* did not require a trap-door.[28] The Folio direction in iv, iii is simply "Enter Barnardine". But the directors who have preferred the trap door entrance have, I think, the root of the matter. Invulnerable to the censor, this figure of the mental underworld forces himself up into the play's consciousness to announce: "I swear I will not die today for any man's persuasion". Nor does he; nor does what he represents.

5 Pattern in *Othello*

The broad problem of all *Othello*-criticism is to reconcile a naturalistic, psychological reading with a symbolic interpretation. This is no doubt true of all the major Shakespearean dramas, but it is particularly true of *Othello*. We have, or appear to have, a fairly clear-cut pattern of good and evil that can be closely identified with the three main personages: that is, of evil, personified in Iago, struggling in the soul of Othello for possession of the good, Desdemona. This pattern, allied to the play's images of heaven and hell, has stimulated a tendency to read *Othello* as a symbolic drama of good overthrown by evil. Thus, we have G. Wilson Knight's interpretation of *Othello* in terms of Christian symbolism,[1] while Irving Ribner has stressed the stock Renaissance figures (the gull, Vice, and so on) out of which the symbolic drama grew.[2] Bernard Spivack, again, in his researches into the ancestral past of Iago, has emphasized the allegorical aspect of the play.[3] This tendency has gone far to modify the older attempts at reading *Othello* in terms of the naturalistic drama. The difficulty is that the symbolic approach may oversimplify the issues of the play. Carried over into actual production, the identification of Iago with Evil, Desdemona with Good, and Othello with Good Overthrown can rob *Othello* of its vitality and plausibility. The difficulties of performance have been confirmed by Wilson Knight, from his experience as a producer: "The symbolic effects are all in the poetry. . . . But the moment any of this is allowed to interfere with the expressly domestic and human qualities of the drama, you get disaster".[4]

The allegory is certainly there. I do not dispute the Christian symbolism of the play: of temptation, by evil and jealousy, and regeneration through love. But the crux is the identification of the symbolic issues with the main actors. I think that *Othello* is indeed about good and evil, but not in any simple sense. The concepts of good and evil are explored in and through human terms. In other words, I believe that we must analyze the play primarily in psychological terms, from which we may then abstract the concepts of good and evil which this play advances. I think it more helpful to assume that conceptualization follows rather than precedes Shakespeare's observation of the empirical data of human behaviour.

I propose here to reopen the question of the psychological drama of *Othello,* and through it arrive at a reassessment of the play's meaning. It is not, however, necessary to follow the usual method of concentration on isolated analysis of character.[5] In this play especially it helps to think in terms of *relationships,* as well as individuals. I shall attempt, accordingly, to isolate the theme of *Othello* by studying the series of relationships through which the play unfolds. The meaning of the play is coded into a recurring situation.

I   IAGO–RODERIGO

The opening presents an immediate situation of disbelief and attempted conviction :

> Tush ! never tell me; I take it much unkindly
> That thou, Iago, who hast had my purse
> As if the strings were thine, shouldst know of this

says Roderigo; and :

> 'Sblood, but you'll not hear me :
> If ever I did dream of such a matter,
> Abhor me

rejoins Iago. Without a moment's delay, the play is properly launched. The first speaker in the play has said, in effect, how can I trust you? And the responder can only seek to convince him, through reference to known facts.

The pattern of the play is clearly prefigured. Iago points to the external and known fact that he has been passed over for promotion, the second-in-command post going to Cassio. It does not follow from this that Roderigo can trust Iago; but at least Iago's ill will to the Moor is established, and that is a ground for trust. But there follows a passage in which Iago concedes to Roderigo the whole truth, as men will to a man they despise :

> In following him, I follow but myself;
> Heaven is my judge, not I for love and duty,
> But seeming so, for my peculiar end :
> For when my outward action does demonstrate
> The native act and figure of my heart
> In compliment extern, 'tis not long after
> But I will wear my heart upon my sleeve
> For daws to peck at : I am not what I am.
>
> (i, i, 58–65)

The will is paramount—a thought to be elaborated later, in i, iii, 322-37; but it cannot be identified. Its nature and true aims must always remain enigmatic; and conviction can only be induced through the rhetoric of persuasion, the appeal to external data. The hollowness of the structure is perfectly revealed to the gull Roderigo, but for the moment he is convinced; he believes what he wants to believe : a thought applied to Othello at the very last (v, ii, 176–7).

II   BRABANTIO–RODERIGO

The action shifts to Brabantio and Roderigo. "What is the reason of this terrible summons?" demands Brabantio, as the alarm is raised. Iago describes in the grossest terms the coupling of Desdemona and Othello; Brabantio concludes that Iago and Roderigo are obscene ruffians. Yet Roderigo, rising for once to the decent and civil address of a gentleman, finds words that carry conviction (i, i, 121–41). He tells Brabantio to examine Desdemona's chamber, to see if she be gone. If she is gone, and if she has her father's permission, well. If not, the rebuke is unmerited.

> If this be known to you and your allowance,
> We then have done you bold and saucy wrongs;
> But if you know not this, my manners tell me
> We have your wrong rebuke.
>
> (i, i, 128–31)

Roderigo refers Brabantio to the "facts" of the case; it has the accent of truth and weight. Brabantio finds his daughter gone, and turns to "good Roderigo" for support, following the "deception" of his daughter. Yet the situation is not what Brabantio thinks.

Roderigo too is attempting to serve his "peculiar end"; and the rebuke of Brabantio is justified. The true distinction between the two sides in the colloquy is focused to the sharp exchange between Brabantio and the hidden Iago :

Brabantio   Thou art a villain.
Iago   You are—a senator.

(I, i, 119)

Brabantio essays a genuine moral comment on the nature and aims of Iago. Iago coolly applies a functional category to Brabantio. A senator is a senator : he holds office : he may be bad or good : we can describe him adequately in terms of what he *does*. Brabantio seeks to define what Iago *is*.

III   OTHELLO–BRABANTIO

The harsh dialogue between Othello and Brabantio intensifies the issue of belief. Brabantio has found that his daughter has secretly married; to that extent he has certainly been deceived, and can regard it as a "treason of the blood" (I, i, 170). He draws a rigid and extreme conclusion : "Fathers, from hence trust not your daughters' minds / By what you see them act" (I, i, 171–2). Only one escape clause is possible, that Desdemona has been overcome by magic. But this notion is blown away by Othello's tale, and Desdemona's calm verification. So, since Desdemona's reasoned defence of the "divided duty" to husband and father is not acceptable, his bitterness is understandable—and, let us admit it, not unjustified. John Wain's reference to Desdemona's "natural guilelessness"[6] does not quite square with the facts of the case.

Othello stands apparently opposed to Brabantio; in fact he shares Brabantio's code of loyalty, and identity of appearance and reality. Almost his first words assert the value for which he stands. Iago advises him to go in, as the "raised father" and his friends approach : Othello is supremely confident :

Not I; I must be found :
My parts, my title and my perfect soul
Shall manifest me rightly . . .

(I, ii, 30–32)

The appearance and the essence form a complete whole. It is a matter not only of temperament, but also of confidence. But that confidence can be undermined, and with it temperament. We have no means of telling how far then and later Othello's belief in Desdemona is undermined initially by Brabantio himself; but the arguments are certainly voiced, and are considerable. There is the matter of racial antipathy : would Desdemona :

> have, t'incur a general mock,
> Run from her guardage to the sooty bosom
> Of such a thing as thou. . . .
>
> (I, ii, 69–71)

The reference to "general mock" makes it clear that the Venetian mores did *not* approve racial intermarriage—a powerful argument to group psychology. Then, her modesty and timidity of spirit are described (I, iii, 94–106). Finally, there is the fatal thrust of Brabantio :

> Look to her, Moor, if thou hast eyes to see :
> She has deceiv'd her father, and may thee.
>
> (I, iii, 293–4)

It is the best of the arguments, and it is not capable in its own terms of refutation; the only counter is pure trust, and that Othello immediately supplies : "My life upon her faith !" (I, iii, 295). He had already desired Desdemona's presence with him at Cyprus, not for her body, but "to be free and bounteous to her mind" (I, iii, 266). As with all romantics, it is the meeting of minds that fascinates Othello. Perhaps he is already subconsciously aware that the appeal to external evidence can go against him.

IV   INTERLUDE : THE ATTACK ON CYPRUS

While these matters of personal relationship are occupying us, Shakespeare advances the theme through the incident of the Turkish attack on Cyprus. A message is brought to the Venetian leaders that the Turkish fleet is bearing on Rhodes. They coldly analyse the news, and reject credence of it, as a feint :

First Senator   This cannot be,
          By no assay of reason : 'tis a pageant,
          To keep us in false gaze : When we consider
          Th'importantcy of Cyprus to the Turk,
          And let ourselves again but understand,
          That as it more concerns the Turk than Rhodes,
          So may he with more facile questions bear it,
          For that it stands not in such warlike brace,
          But altogether lacks th'abilities
          That Rhodes is dress'd in. . . .
                                             (I, iii, 17–26)

They are right : the Turkish objective is Cyprus. Now what is the point of this military miniature? It is not in Cinthio, and is a genuinely Shakespearean piece of business. It hardly adds to the theatrical excitement of the crisis, and apparently slows up the real action. Its purpose is to maintain the theme before the audience, and demonstrate by contrast the capacity, so unlike Othello's, to weigh and sift evidence and from it deduce the workings of the mind. It has been said that had Hamlet been in Othello's position, he could readily have solved the problem. But Hamlet's lucid analysis of motivation is perfectly well illustrated in this play by the subtle Venetians. The Venetian leader represents admirably the character of his people when, in reply to Brabantio's wild allegations, he says :

                To vouch this, is no proof,
          Without more wider and more overt test
          Than these thin habits and poor likelihoods
          Of modern seeming do prefer against him.
                                             (I, iii, 106–9)

And the consecutive incidents of the Council's business figure to us the play's main affair—the determining of truth upon a just consideration of all available evidence.

V   IAGO–OTHELLO

The main action of the play is now launched, the decisive unfolding of the Iago–Othello relationship. It is not necessary to follow in detail the turns of their relationship, but the main features can readily be abstracted. They turn, however, on the question of Iago's motivation: and this *locus classicus* must briefly be revisited.

Iago himself offers us at least two excellent motives: he has been passed over for promotion (this to Roderigo, a public statement); and he suspects Emilia of adultery (alluded to several times, in private and in public). The jealousy concept is capable of considerable refinement; it need not be accepted in the same terms as Iago gives it us.[7] Heilman accepts that jealousy, in a very broad sense, is the motive; "Iago's jealousy is indeed pervasive"; this for him can more properly be termed *invidia*, or envy.[8] In addition, Bradley's brilliant analysis pointed to an unmentioned motive, a love of power and of manipulating others.[9] These are the main motives on which critics have dwelt and which must be mentioned here; other, peripheral motives need not concern us. Finally, Spivack's study related Iago to the theatrical past of the villain-figure. Concentrating on the pregnant "and" in "I hate the Moor; / And it is thought abroad, that 'twixt my sheets / H'as done my office" (I, iii, 392–4), he identifies certain passages of Iago's as being, in naturalistic terms, unmotivated. In the tradition of Aaron, Don John, Richard of Gloucester, Iago is simply "a villain", as the First Folio designated him. Iago, therefore, is like the others "the hybrid product of two conventions that met and merged in him" (Spivack, p. 47), and the "and" is the "seam between the drama of allegory and the drama of nature" (Spivack, p. 448).

The issues, then, for all writers on *Othello* come down to these. Can Iago's account of his motives be trusted? Alternatively, can we extend them, relying on the truism that people do not understand themselves, and that Iago's account of himself may require either rejection or elaboration? Or do we regard Iago as a figure (either heavily symbolic or tradition-shaped) that cannot be assessed in naturalistic terms at all?

The third possibility is crucial, and needs to be taken first. I do not believe that Shakespeare, at the height of his powers, created a single personage who could not be accepted as an entirely credible human being. And we have a simple device to counter the compelling evidence of Iago's past (for there is no gainsaying that a quantity of traditional material has been assimilated into Iago's speeches). We may say that Iago is consciously alluding to the Vice-figure, consciously and delightedly modelling himself on the Villain. "And what's he then that says I play the villain?" This is of the same order as the grotesquely exaggerated hell-imagery in his speeches, which we should not take at face value. Iago, in truth, likes to think of himself as evil, as the villain; he plays the role in capital letters. It is braggadocio, part of his pose, the performance that he acts for his own benefit. It has been a commonplace of *Othello*-criticism since Hazlitt that Iago is an artist in evil; it is true, and the art is acting. Shakespeare got away with his problem by introducing a strong element of role-playing into Iago's make-up that explains and exculpates the traditional material.

This settled, the first two issues can now be considered. They can be regarded as composing together a spectrum, with no clear division, along which the majority of modern critics place themselves. At one end of the spectrum we have the solid, unshakeable view of Sprague: "Iago's motives are expounded in his soliloquies".[10] Kittredge concurs: "He is actuated by resentment for injustice . . . this motive is not only human (that is, neither monstrous nor maniacal), but has a kind of foundation in reason and justice."[11] So: "Iago's account of the matter must be accepted as substantially true" (Kittredge, p. 119). There is, to my mind, no arguing with the main thesis here. The soliloquy has, for Elizabethan playwrights and audiences, the force of a moral absolute. It is not to be questioned. And one can only wonder at the enviable lives of critics who can airily wave aside so fragile a motive as being passed over in favour of a better man. As Laurence Olivier, drawing on his wartime experiences, has pointed out: "The fact of rank and its distinctions could quite frequently be found to be as justifiable a basis for Iago's bitterness as any".[12] Nevertheless, a respect for Iago's stated motives is not incompatible with a belief that he has others. This leads us to the other half of the spectrum, at the end of which stands Bradley. For him, all Iago's statements are to be treated with the utmost reserve. The real motive, nowhere mentioned, is a love of power. Now, as a principle of Shakespearean interpretation one ought to be as little as possible exclusive. One can suggest a sort of reverse Occam's razor here, that entities ought not to be rejected unnecessarily. I believe in the validity of Iago's stated motives; and I believe in the power-complex theory too. I can have both, and I want both. It seems to me perfectly in order to accept that soliloquies represent conventionally the actual thoughts of a speaker, and to accept that his verbalized thoughts may yet hint at deep-lying impulses that find no explicit outlet in words. Such a view leads to complexities of logic and meaning that have yet to be formulated satisfactorily; the most helpful guides, perhaps, are not the psychoanalysts, but Sartre, in his pages on "Self-deception", and Stanislavsky on subtext. But I can see no major difficulty with the view, sensibly applied, that soliloquies both reveal motive directly and hint at unspoken motive. A major playwright can allow actor and audience a wide range of options.

This preamble is necessary before I can state what seems to me the main point of the Iago–Othello relationship: they share a common motivation, distrust of their wives. I accord considerable weight to Iago's several pronouncements on this matter, and would indeed suggest two basic principles of Iago-interpretation. (1) Believe everything he says, in soliloquy. (2) Accept that in public Iago will tell *as much of the truth as he possibly can*. It is, after all, his method to allude to matter "probal to thinking". Only fools lie unnecessarily, and Iago is not a fool. Bradley has tended, I feel, to misjudge the issue here. Iago is not a liar: he is a deceiver. His speciality is false interpretations of factual data, not lies related to external data which can be exposed. I offer as a commentary on Iago, Talleyrand's distinction between Metternich and Mazarin: "*Le Cardinal trompait; mais il ne mentait pas. Or M. de Metternich ment toujours, et ne trompe jamais*". I believe Iago, therefore, when he says that he suspects his wife with Othello:

> I hate the Moor:
> And it is thought abroad, that 'twixt my sheets
> H'as done my office: I know not if't be true;
> But I, for mere suspicion in that kind,
> Will do as if for surety.
>
> (i, iii, 392–6)

He repeats it (ii, i, 304–8): Emilia alludes to it (iv, ii, 145–7): and in two passages of sexual innuendo, that I shall discuss later, the matter is hinted at. I shall argue later that a case of sorts for Iago's suspicions is present within the framework of the play (and *not* in its imaginative hinterland, after the manner of some old-time critics). For the moment I simply emphasize that Iago and Othello both distrust their wives' chastity, and have no means of proving it.

Othello and Iago thus share an involvement with a general problem. The problem is the same one throughout *Othello*: to come at the workings of the human mind. Iago, quite correctly—his capacity for telling the truth is his strongest weapon—argues that only circumstantial evidence is possible :

> But yet, I say,
> If imputation and strong circumstances,
> Which lead directly to the door of truth,
> Will give you satisfaction, you may have't.
>
> (III, iii, 405–8)

All possible circumstantial evidence is paraded. There is the suspicious slinking-away of Cassio, followed by Desdemona's advocacy of him; the habits of the Venetian ladies (III, iii, 201–4); the deception of her father, a point which then raised by Iago yields an immediate "and so she did" from Othello (III, iii, 208); the business of the handkerchief; and over all the personal testimony of Iago. Now this evidence as presented is not only in the obvious sense a confidence trick; it is also, in the philosophic sense, a confidence trick, an illogical argument. For the lynch-pin of the circumstantial evidence is Iago's testimony; and Iago's testimony is only good because he is trusted; but then so is Desdemona. Why should trust be overthrown by trust?

For Othello is a creature made for trust. His world-order is based on it :

> But I do love thee! and when I love thee not,
> Chaos is come again.
>
> (III, iii, 91–2)

And above all, "Men should be what they seem" (III, iii, 128)—echoing, of all people, Iago. The defection of Desdemona is more than a personal loss, it is demolition of a philosophy of existence. It is noteworthy that when Othello in his anguish cries out, it is for *certainty,* above all—not the reassurance of baseless suspicious, but the truth, however ugly :

> Villain, be sure thou prove my love a whore,
> Be sure of it; give me the ocular proof; . . .
> Make me to see't, or, at the least, so prove it,
> That the probation bear no hinge nor loop
> To hang a doubt on; or woe upon thy life !
>
> (III, iii, 359–60, 365–7)

Certainty is his goal. My question, then, remains to be answered at the end: on what grounds does Othello allow his world-order to be overturned, since trust can only be overthrown by trust?

I do not propose to examine in detail the course of the Desdemona–Othello relationship, since its lines are conditioned by the Iago–Othello relationship. It is patent that Desdemona is all trust, that she would never betray her husband. Proof, if it were needed, comes when she absolutely refuses to entertain even theoretically the notion of such a wrong: "Beshrew me, if I would do such a wrong / For the whole world" (IV, iii, 78–9). The audience must take such a statement as an absolute; to doubt it is to doubt the whole import and meaning of *Othello*. Both Othello and Desdemona depend absolutely upon the value of trust; only she is consistent: she resists the perhaps playful, but nonetheless seductive temptations of Emilia, a scene that parallels structurally her husband's undermining of Othello in III, iii.

VI   IAGO–RODERIGO (CONTINUED)

Iago's relationship with Roderigo persists throughout the play, forming an intermittent structural parallel with the other relationships; and it should at least form a corrective to the idea that *Othello* is a play about jealousy. Roderigo, for all that he is a gull, has the sense to doubt Iago—he is the only one in the play to do so—and brings out the clearest illustrations of Iago's views and methods. He persuades Roderigo of Desdemona's fondness for Cassio (II, i, 220–53): "a pestilent complete knave, and the woman has found him already". This is by reference to the external facts of the youth, proximity, and attractiveness of Cassio and Desdemona. They obviously are attracted, and Iago coolly sums up the matter in private:

> That Cassio loves her, I do well believe't;
> That she loves him, 'tis apt and of great credit.
>
> (II, i, 294–5)

The evidence of action resides merely in the fulsome kissing of hands, however. Later Roderigo makes his most determined push against his tormentor: "your words and performances are no kin together" (IV, ii, 184–5). This is the right approach, but Iago is allowed to wriggle out of it with more words, not action; Roderigo is set to kill Cassio. This he agrees to unwillingly : "And yet he hath given me satisfying reasons" (v, i, 9). The value of trust yields to the rhetoric of persuasion. The point to make is that intellectually the argument between Iago and Roderigo parallels exactly that between Iago and Othello.

VII   IAGO—CASSIO

The situation of disbelief and conviction contains some interesting variations in Iago's relationship with Cassio. The essence is that Iago, if not positively distrusted, is kept at his distance. Several possible reasons support Cassio's aloofness. First, he is in that delicate organizational situation, when he has beaten a rival to a promotion, but still needs to work with him and be on civil (but not familiar) terms; there is usually an element of distrust, of insecurity, in this position. Second, there are hints that Iago comes from a lower social stratum than Cassio, and in the drinking scene Cassio's references to "man of quality" and "the lieutenant is to be saved before the ancient" suggest an element of class antagonism, or at least a desire to stress superior rank. Then there is the strictly functional element of the situation : there is a case for saying that in an organization no superior should wholly trust his subordinate. At all events, we see Iago, of all people, deceived in Act I, scene ii, when Cassio feigns total ignorance of Othello's wooing and marriage. It is perfectly proper for Cassio to know no more than he is officially supposed to know, yet this indication that he is not prepared to confide in his subordinate has its human significance. And the deception is turned against him by Iago, at the beginning of the great temptation scene. Everything to Iago is evidence.

A further hint of the distrust is supplied in the interchange between Othello and Cassio at the beginning of II, iii. Othello, as the wise—and tactful—general, puts it to Cassio :

> Good Michael, look you to the guard to-night :
> Let's teach ourselves that honourable stop,
> Not to outsport discretion.
>
> (II, iii, 1–3)

—a discreet reference, surely, to Cassio's known weakness with the bottle. Cassio prefers not to take this to himself, but like a good subordinate passes the word down:

> Iago hath direction what to do;
> But, notwithstanding, with my personal eye
> Will I look to't.
>
> (II, iii, 4–6)

Again, the reply is most proper: but is there not a hint here that Iago would be as well overseen? Othello chimes in with the kindly and reassuring "Iago is most honest" (II, iii, 7)—a tactful reminder, perhaps, that Cassio has a good man under him, whom it would be as well to be on good terms with. The passage has a bafflingly pellucid opacity, typically Shakespearean: but the hint is there, to be brought out in production if required (otherwise, the passage calls for no comment, as a simple piece of military routine).

Cassio remains, however, notably reserved. Iago enters a moment later and tries to engage his superior in some sexual speculation on the prowess of Desdemona. Cassio refuses to be drawn, and his cold, trustless answers maintain the distance. Not until Cassio's disgrace, and Iago's apparent attempts to help him, is the barrier broken down. Then, for the first time (as Empson points out) Cassio calls him "honest Iago" (II, iii, 341). The reversal of rank puts their human relationship on a much better footing, as it appears: "I never knew / A Florentine more kind and honest", wonders Cassio (III, i, 42–3). Thereafter Cassio freely accepts Iago's advice and help, convinced by the fact that it is (objectively) extremely good. To seek Desdemona's support is the best possible advice. Here again we encounter the problem of external data: that it is all that mankind has to go upon, yet it needs interpretation, without which it is meaningless.

In sum, then, Cassio–Iago is a further, if delicate exploration of trust and conviction, based this time on the ambiguities of the subordinate–superior relationship—one which necessitates a tension of human and functional requirements. It is intensified by an opposition of social class, conversational address, and sexual attractiveness that brings out in each man an awareness of insecurity: most revealingly in Iago, with his muttered:

> if Cassio do remain,
> He hath a daily beauty in his life
> That makes me ugly; . . .
>   (v, i, 18–20)

In fact, this category of relationship is quite as difficult to assess as the sexual category; and Shakespeare has sketched an unwritten play in this miniature study.

VIII   CASSIO–BIANCA

An echo of the main plot-situation occurs in the Cassio–Bianca relationship. We have (in effect) three husband–wife situations in *Othello,* just as there are three father–son relationships in *Hamlet.* Bianca's passion for her lover Cassio is lightly sketched in, but with sexes reversed the situation clearly forms a variant of Othello–Desdemona and Iago–Emilia. Act iii, scene iv, gives us the essence of the matter, and we hardly need Cassio's additional comments to Iago in the following scene. Bianca loves, but does not trust; for the excellent reason that Cassio's man-of-the-world relationship with her does not admit of a reciprocal love. On this basic mistrust two facts precipitate a scene: Cassio's week-long absence from her house, and the display of Desdemona's handkerchief. The matter is not enlarged on in the play, and need not detain us here; but we can see it as a further variation of the main theme, which is *not* the passion of jealousy, but the problem of which jealousy is the symptom.

IX   IAGO–EMILIA

We come now to what is, in terms of the intellectual argument, the most important relationship in the play. It has been neglected by recent critics, and that is perhaps strange since, although the relationship occupies far less space in the play than Othello–Desdemona, it is the determinant of that relationship. We are told on several occasions, directly and indirectly, that Iago distrusts his wife, and that this is a mainspring of his campaign against Othello. What, then, is the nature of this relationship that generates the main action of the play?

Bradley dismissed out of hand the interpretation of Iago as "an ordinary villain . . . a husband who believes he has been wronged, and will make his enemy suffer a jealousy worse than his own . . ." (p. 170). This, for him, was a false interpretation, if better than the "lunacies" of supposing, for example, that Othello *did* seduce Emilia. I believe this to be an altogether too cavalier dismissal of the dominant aspect of the Emilia–Iago relationship.

Part of the evidence I have already alluded to. Iago, in soliloquy, twice refers directly and strongly to his fears that Othello has cuckolded him (i, iii, 392–6; ii, i, 304–8). He passingly suspects even Cassio (ii, i, 316). In two further passages he alludes to his wife's sexual appetite, an idea that relates easily to his fears of her chastity. Thus, with Desdemona present, he tells her, "you rise to play, and go to bed to work": an ambivalent, but apparently pleasant enough jest, reminiscent of the Antonio–Duchess dialogue in *The Duchess of Malfi* (iii, ii, 23–6), and in tune with the mask of blunt good fellowship he normally assumes. Later, in an occasion when he is alone with his wife, Iago offers her what is virtually a direct example of the affront sexual (and one not mentioned by Bradley):

> *Emilia*   Do not you chide; I have a thing for you.
> *Iago*   A thing for me? It is a common thing—
> *Emilia*   Ha?
> *Iago*   To have a foolish wife.
>
> (iii, iii, 301–4)

In the general context of the Elizabethan drama, to call "common thing" a double entendre is simply misleading: it means one thing only.

Iago's jealousy of his wife, then, is established beyond all reasonable doubt. But what are his grounds? Emilia herself rejects his fears as groundless, to his face:

> *Emilia*   O fie upon them! Some such squire he was
>   That turn'd your wit the seamy side without,
>   And made you to suspect me with the Moor.
>
> (iv, ii, 145–7)

This utterance lies at the core of the play's meaning; or rather, we can trace the play's meaning thus far, until it disappears into the sands. Here the clue to human conduct ends. *Who was Iago's Iago?* We are not told. We do do not know whether he existed, what arguments he used, or whether Iago's own brain spawned the distrust. On the great question of the determination of human action, Shakespeare offers us a wide range of data—and then declines to impose a priority. Any conclusions reached will be our own, not Shakespeare's.

Nevertheless, the matter is probed further, in the fascinating dialogue between Desdemona and Emilia in iv, iii, 61–106. Our whole response to the play should be conditioned by our reading of that dialogue. Desdemona asks simply :

> Dost thou in conscience think,—tell me, Emilia,—
> That there be woman do abuse their husbands
> In such gross kind ?
>
> (iv, iii, 61–3)

We note the careful, balanced, give-nothing-away response of Emilia : "There be some such, no doubt" : the turning of Desdemona's question "Woudst thou do such a deed, for all the world?" with "Why, would not you?" And then, after the jockeying for position, the confidences begin to flow : Desdemona would not, Emilia would. She tells us so :

Desdemona	No, by this heavenly light !
Emilia	Nor I neither by this heavenly light;
	I might do't as well i'the dark.
Desdemona	Wouldst thou do such a deed for all the world?
Emilia	The world's a huge thing : it is a great price
	For a small vice.

(iv, iii, 65–9)

Not for a small thing, but for a great thing, Emilia would do it : she elaborates the thought (72–7). It has the ring of half-earnest, half-jest. Then in her final speech what seems like the truth comes through : it has all the accent of honest indignation, and the shift from prose to verse is vital :

> But I do think it is their husbands' faults
> If wives do fall : say that they slack their duties,
> And pour our treasures into foreign laps.

> Or else break out in peevish jealousies,
> Throwing restraint upon us; or say they strike us,
> Or scant our former having in despite;
> Why, we have galls, and though we have some grace,
> Yet have we some revenge. Let husbands know
> Their wives have sense like them : they see and smell
> And have their palates both for sweet and sour
> As husbands have. What is it that they do
> When they change us for others? Is it sport?
> I think it is : and doth affection breed it?
> I think it doth : is't frailty that thus errs?
> It is so too : and have not we affections,
> Desires for sport, and frailty, as men have?
> Then let them use us well : else let them know,
> The ills we do, their ills instruct us so.
>
> (IV, iii, 87–104)

Here we locate one of the cruces of the play. It is hardly possible for a reader of any sensibility to deny that here, using general terms, Emilia is speaking of herself. *She* puts the whole onus upon husbands; they are jealous, they ill-use wives, play around with other women. Is it not fair return for wives to seek consolation with other men?

It may be, indeed. But where is the truth of the matter? Iago has claimed that Emilia played him false. Emilia says, in effect, that it would be no more than fair *if* she did. And here we realize that we have stumbled upon the play's true situation : it is a sexual square-dance, in which the mutual distrusts of Iago and Emilia activate and parallel the relationship between Othello and Desdemona. It is not possible to apportion blame to Iago and Emilia. For myself, I believe we can dismiss the fantasy of an Othello–Emilia intrigue : there is not a scrap of evidence beyond Iago's statement. But we cannot dismiss the possibility of Emilia's adultery *with someone else*—with anyone who would conveniently fill the role of wife's revenge. This possibility need not relate to the past : it can be entertained as a future event. It is not, I think, a foolishly hypothetical speculation. One can only agree with L. C. Knights that we know about the characters "only what the play requires us to know". We know nothing about Emilia's actual adultery, if any. We do know that within the framework of *Othello* it is presented to us as a strong possibility. It is not necessary to prove that

Emilia has actually committed adultery—with Othello, or with anyone else. It is sufficient to prove that she was actually entertaining the idea. And for that, no proof is required beyond Emilia's word, which we have.

What we have, therefore, is a perfectly commonplace marital situation, in which mutual distrust feeds on possibilities of past or future betrayals. Iago, the man of supreme sexual scepticism, has a valid ground for doubt; his wife, as he would readily apprehend, is *at least* contemplating the prospect of taking a lover, if she has not already done so. We know that Iago suspects Emilia : we know that he has openly challenged her : we know that she resents it. The situation thus created is in essence self-perpetuating and self-justifying. To say this is not to take sides with either partner; nor should one. It is curious to note the ambivalence even of Bradley here, who tells us : "One must constantly remember not to believe a syllable that Iago utters on any subject", until tested (p. 172); while offering "a word of warning against critics who take her [Emilia's] light talk too seriously" (p. 197). This is sheer sentimentalism. It is sentimental to believe in Emilia's virtue, against her own word to the contrary, while disbelieving Iago's own motivation, though partially confirmed by Emilia's words. The fact is that Iago and Emilia have strong grounds for mutual distrust : which are, that they are married to each other.

To sum up here, I do not, naturally, regard Emilia and Iago as essentially on the same level. Emilia is a goodhearted creature, who under normal circumstances would adhere to the wifely ethic. But under the stress of living with Iago's suspicions, her morale has clearly deteriorated. Iago, for his part, tends to see life in the simplest of biological terms, and is ready to accredit everyone—including his wife—with the most primitive mainsprings of conduct. This tendency would be confirmed by Emilia's reaction to his own behaviour. It is impossible that we sift the matter to the origin; the first act of distrust-causation, on either side, we can never know. And it is impossible that we know the true facts of the later development of the case; whether Emilia did betray, or might have betrayed, Iago is not established. Only the possibility is there, though quite distinctly maintained before us by Shakespeare.

X   OTHELLO–DESDEMONA

We can now properly interpret the major relationship of the play in terms of the minor; for, as I hold, the Emilia–Iago relationship provides the core of the play. I earlier raised the question of Othello: why should trust be overthrown by trust? Only one satisfactory answer can be given, and it is provided by Iago, at the very end. In reply to his wife's agonized entreaty to deny his responsibility for the tragedy, he tells as much of the truth as he can combine with his sliding position:

> I told him what I thought, and told no more
> Than what he found himself was apt and true.
>
> (v, ii, 176–7)

It is the truth: Iago's epitaph on Othello—and on himself. Othello's trust in his wife was overthrown, because he did not trust her.

There is a sufficiency of hints to point this way. Quite early, in a moment of triumph, we have the faint breath of a fear:

> *Othello*   If it were now to die,
> 'Twere now to be most happy; for, I fear,
> My soul hath her content so absolute
> That not another comfort like to this
> Succeeds in unknown fate.
>
> (ii, i, 191–5)

Again, there is the negative hint, a moment before the turning of the play's tide, in "But I do love thee! and when I love thee not, / Chaos is come again" (iii, iii, 91–2). These faint straws point strongly one way when Iago begins his work. It is relatively easy: Othello fairly wrenches the disclosure out of Iago. "Indeed: discern'st thou aught in that? Is he not honest?" (iii, iii, 102–3). Why should Othello question Cassio's honesty, the first to do so? Why does he not send Iago about his business once the matter is openly raised? Why does he not once seriously move to his wife's defence? The temptation scene can only make dramatic and psychological sense if it is plainly understood that Othello is not a pure innocent subverted by Iago: he has already entertained suspicions ("some monster", "too hideous", 107–8) that are brought to the light with rapidity and ease by Iago.[14]

In this sense chiefly can Iago be regarded as a symbol of evil; he embodies the evil in Othello, is successful only because he can evoke a response in Othello parallel to his own variety of evil. Othello's sin is Iago's sin : distrust, the force of disintegration, and chaos. The tragedy of Othello is not that he kills his wife; that is the mere dramatic and emotional consequence of his sin. It is that he voluntarily overturns his whole world-order, based on trust : "Chaos is come again".

My analysis of *Othello* has elucidated chiefly a situation, a relationship, a character, and a concept of evil. Let us review them.

The business of *Othello* is the relationship between human behaviour and human motivation, between words and thoughts, actions and purposes. The constant preoccupation of the play is the problem : how, given the external data of behaviour, can one relate it to the minds of the actors? This problem, applied to Othello and Desdemona, is in the forefront of the play, and therefore creates the misleading impression that the play is about jealousy. But it is not : jealousy is simply a consequence, in certain sexual situations, of a failure to resolve this general human problem. And in the terms in which I have defined it, the problem is debated by Roderigo, Brabantio, Iago, Cassio, Bianca, Emilia, and the Venetian leaders. The answer to the problem, in human terms, can only be made thus : that trust, arrived at after a full intuitive and intellectual grasp of the data, should be an absolute value. The intuitive, and intellectual, models are Desdemona and the Venetian leaders—to one of whom is allotted the play's final cadence.

The relationship that best embodies this theme is Emilia and Iago. That is because it is causal to the main action of the play. We have each side of the relationship sufficiently presented to us : deep suspicion on Iago's part, resentment, and readiness to justify suspicion, on Emilia's. The facts of the case are inscrutable with regard to the origin and development of the mutual distrust; but the situation, within the limits presented to us, is clear. The marriage stands badly, notwithstanding Emilia's still-present affection for her "wayward husband". The Iago–Emilia relationship, moreover, is not only causal to the play's main action; it is paradigmatic to the play's main theme. We know, after all, the main facts of the Othello–Desdemona case. We do not know the facts concerning Emilia and her husband. Their relationship is an enigma standing at the heart of the play's mystery. Since I see the unresolvable appearance–reality dualism as the centre of the *Othello* design, I regard Emilia–Iago as the play's central relationship.

If anywhere, the origins of this situation must be looked to in the character of Iago. He is active, Emilia passive. Emilia has sketched in a reactive philosophy, in iv, iii, 87–104, while Iago has stated a philosophy of will, in i, iii, 322–37. Therefore we must take Iago as the senior member of the partnership, and the focus of the problems of human behaviour examined in *Othello*. On Iago, Shakespeare, though he provides us with much data, provides no conclusion: Iago's curtain lines are a perfectly consistent extension of his philosophy of the unidentifiable human will, or essence:

> Demand me nothing: what you know, you know:
> From this time forth I never will speak word.
>
> (v, ii, 303–4)

Shakespeare has outlined his case and will go no further; he tosses the problem of Iago, and with it the whole play, into our laps, to decide as we can. What are we to make of Iago, and the problems he embodies?

Since Iago makes perfectly good sense as a psychological and naturalistic study, I cannot see him as the Satanic figure of Irving Ribner and other writers. Wilson Knight, while accepting Iago as a devil-symbol, lodges the formidable caveat quoted earlier. The mass of evidence of stage performances compiled by Marvin Rosenberg confirms this judgment. Iago, played as Evil, fails. He must be played as a human being, and it is the task of the critic to analyse his evil from that point of departure. In other words, Heilman is exactly right in his caution: "If we start by simply calling Iago a 'devil' we risk using the myth of evil as a substitute for the analysis of the individual. . . . What goes on in the play is less to be defined by than to define *devil*" (p. 42).

What, then, is the nature of Iago's devilry? We may be inclined to accept Miss Bodkin's interpretation of Iago's devilry:

> If we attempt to define the devil in psychological terms,
> regarding him as an archetype, a persistent or recurrent mode of
> apprehension, we may say that the devil is our tendency to

represent in personal form the forces within and without us that threaten our supreme values.[15]

This seems to me acute and true, but we can distinguish between Iago-in-Othello and Iago himself. Iago himself is not Evil; he is merely criminal. He is a perfectly well-known criminal type—cold, egocentric, callous rather than sadistic. In the design of the play he stands for a particular evil—distrust, the most corrosive of emotions. He is not unique in the possession of this evil, for Othello too demonstrates it. Iago's awareness of the unknowability of the human soul has led him to a conclusion that is untenable—the over-riding need of the predatory, trustless human will to satisfy itself against all humanity. And that way chaos lies. For Iago's sin is to have seen the truth, and drawn false conclusions from it. No human being can resolve the duality of behaviour and mind. But a *modus vivendi* must be found between human beings, else society becomes, in Spivack's phrase, "the arena of endless competition, more or less organized, between the appetites of one man and another" (p. 424). In *Othello* the primal sin is that of the man who—actuated by pangs of envy, jealousy, thwarted ambition, and a complex of related motives—fastens on to the brute facts of an insoluble human problem and uses them to destroy this *modus vivendi*.

And it is too simple to infer of Shakespeare's design that "evil operates through deception".[16] It may indeed do so; but so may good. To suggest an absolute coupling of evil with deception is to overlook Sonnet XCIV :

> They that have pow'r to hurt and will do none,
> That do not do the thing they most do show,
> Who, moving others, are themselves as stone,
> Unmoved, cold, and to temptation slow,
> They rightly do inherit heaven's graces
> And husband nature's riches from expense;
> They are the lords and owners of their faces,
> Others but stewards of their excellence.

To dissociate appearance from essence may be praiseworthy—if the end is good. And we have Henry V as the case in point. Bradley's description of Iago—"a thoroughly bad, *cold* man"—can be reversed for Henry, a good, cold man. In the Shakespearean canon of values, it is not only Evil that knows how to hide its face.

We come, then, to a final attack on the problem of *Othello* : and that is not the inscrutability of evil, as such, but the inscrutability of the human soul. The last effective word is Iago's : "Demand me nothing, what you know, you know." This is a final and definitive statement, not only on Iago, but on every other personage in the play. It is the authentic Shakespearean voice, and the verdict enshrines a philosophy of life and of dramaturgy. The essence of the Shakespearean concept of character is not to make absolute statements, but to provide a range of behavioural data—words, and actions—on which a final interpretation (which is never forthcoming) can be based. To reject Iago as impossibly evil is to overlook the wide range of Iago's ideas that are essentially Shakespeare's own.

6 *Macbeth:* the Sexual Underplot

The centrality of *desire* and *act* in *Macbeth* is obvious enough, and has received its due of recognition.[1] I want here to concentrate on the deep ambivalence of these terms: that is, their impregnation with sexual and non-sexual meanings. Nothing need be said of the "innocent" senses of these terms. They are the material of everyday discourse, and need no commentary. But the course of the action suggests a sexual colouration, which itself indicates a perspective on the psychology of Macbeth and Lady Macbeth and thus on the archetypal action of the drama. In this, Shakespeare is I think following the linguistic strategy of *Measure for Measure,* in which a number of generally "innocent" terms are increasingly seen to bear a heavily sexual charge, until finally all becomes explicit in the Duke's proposal of marriage. But in *Macbeth,* the action around which the sexual meanings cluster occurs early: killing the King. It is to this action that our inquiry into the sexual vibrations of the piece must be directed.

Macbeth's early invocation "Stars, hide your fires; / Let not light see my black and deep desires" (I, iv, 50–1) initiates the sequence. On it, Jorgensen comments: "The 'black and deep desires'—an expression which by its vagueness enhances the terrible sense of obscure evil—are not to be exposed to the light of moral vocabulary".[2] It is precisely this obscurity (Jorgensen well describes it as a linguistic characteristic of the play)[3] that creates a kind of imaginative hinterland in which meanings can breed. Here, the association of "desire" with "night" and (implied) "shame" is at least interesting. Macbeth's letter to his wife phrases his impulse a little more provocatively: "When I burned in desire to question them further . . ." (I, v, 3–4). This scene then clarifies into Lady Macbeth's great invocation, "Come, you spirits / That tend on mortal thoughts, unsex me here" (I, v, 41–2) and the sexual presence in the play becomes overt.

It is manifest in the encounter between Macbeth and his wife later in the scene. As a general rule in Shakespeare, linguistic meanings cannot adequately be considered in a lexical vacuum. The words are charged with meanings by theatre itself. And here, the stage context is the meeting, and the relationship between Macbeth and Lady Macbeth. It is, of course, unnecessary today to dispose of the idea that Lady Macbeth is a stage virago, a repellent termagant. That was a cliché of stage practice—indeed, an historic aberration—that has now been allowed to lapse.[4] There is no textual reason whatever to doubt the mien and attraction of the "Fair and noble hostess", as Duncan calls here (I, vi, 24). With her, Macbeth is on terms of deep intimacy and regard. Other indications aside, the terms of address are decisive. "My dearest partner of greatness" is in Macbeth's letter (I, v, 12–13), and his first words on greeting her are "My dearest love" (I, v, 59). Moreover, when Duncan says:

> but he rides well;
> And his great love, sharp as his spur, hath holp him
> To his home before us.
>
> (I, vi, 22–4)

he leaves it tactfully open as to whether "love" refers to Macbeth's solicitude for Duncan, or his desire to greet his wife. The latter possibility is scarcely dispelled by Duncan's reference to "Fair and noble hostess", which follows immediately. The intimacy between Macbeth and his wife is the fundamental stage fact, on which all the sexual possibilities in the language of the two are based.

These possibilities arise almost immediately in their dialogue. Lady Macbeth's imposition of will over her husband has a subtext of sexual suasion:

> He that's coming
> Must be provided for: and you shall put
> This night's great business into my dispatch;
> Which shall to all our nights and days to come
> Give solely sovereign sway and masterdom.
>
> (I, v, 67–71)

This, following the sequence *beguile, bear welcome in your eye, Your hand, your tongue,* reads like a veiled sexual promise. Why "nights"? And why the order, "nights *and days*"? But it is in the great encounter of I, vii that these possibilities arise in their most concentrated and striking form.

Macbeth's soliloquy ends in:

> I have no spur
> To prick the sides of my intent, but only
> Vaulting ambition, which o'erleaps itself
> And falls on th' other.
>
> (I, vi, 25–8)

There is a generally available sexual symbolism in riding, to be invoked or ignored as occasion warrants. Sometimes Shakespeare makes open use of the symbolism, as in *Henry V* (the pre-Agincourt dialogue in the French camp, III, vi, 46–62) and *Antony and Cleopatra* ("Ride on the pants triumphing", IV, viii, 16). Often an explicit reference to riding has no symbolic value whatever, since it is a necessary observation of literal fact. Here, Macbeth's language is totally metaphoric (there is no formal necessity for alluding to riding) so there is free play for associations. These, beginning with "spur", hark back to Duncan's "great love, sharp as his spur"; and the whole sequence of "spur", "prick", "vaulting", "o'erleaps", "falls on th' other" has a repeated sexual reference. The soliloquy is interrupted at this point in the most significant of timings:

> *Enter* Lady Macbeth.

There follows Macbeth's attempt to back off, and Lady Macbeth's counter. Her speech demands quotation in its entirety:

> Was the hope drunk
> Wherein you dress'd yourself? hath it slept since?
> And wakes it now, to look so green and pale
> At what it did so freely? From this time
> Such I account thy love. Art thou afeard
> To be the same in thine own act and valour
> As thou art in desire? Wouldst thou have that
> Which thou esteem'st the ornament of life,
> And live a coward in thine own esteem,
> Letting 'I dare not' wait upon 'I would,'
> Like the poor cat i'the adage?
>
> (35–45)

Her rhetoric is imbued with sexuality, and it preconditions the mode of judgment in which Macbeth perceives the enterprise. Consider the sequence: "drunk", "dress'd", "slept", "wakes" suggest purely a carousal; but "At what it did so freely" begins to insinuate a sexual possibility into the revel. "Such I account thy love" immediately links this metaphoric possibility with his feelings for her —and, moreover, leaves open the extent of the parallelism initiated by "Such". Is "thy love" a continuous state of feeling, or an act? The ambiguity meets, as it seems, its resolution in the next line, "To be the same in thine own act and valour / As thou art in desire". Clearly, "act" carries over some of the sexual energy in "love" (and is reinforced by "desire") while simultaneously affirming the sense of *action*. "Act" is always a chameleon word, and here is coloured by the sexual potential present throughout the speech. The subtextual wave laps around everything hereabouts: I am not even convinced that "ornament of life" refers so unequivocally to the crown as commentators assume.

The general sense of the passage has long been recognized. "Lady Macbeth", as D. W. Harding observes, "commits him to the role not of manhood, but of what she imagines manhood should be".[5] It is the business of *Macbeth* to parse the word *man* exhaustively, and the dialogue here turns on a perfectly clear if unstated sense of the word:

Macbeth	Prithee, peace:
	I dare do all that may become a man;
	Who dares do more is none.
Lady Macbeth	What beast was't, then,
	That made you break this enterprise to me?
	When you durst do it, then you were a man;
	And, to be more than what you were, you would
	Be so much more the man.

(45–51)

A man acts: and *action* is validated by the sexual approval of his mate. Macbeth's perception of the event is deeply coloured by the vision, and the person, of his wife. And she clinches her argument thus:

> when in swinish sleep
> Their drenched natures lie as in a death,
> What cannot you and I perform upon
> Th' unguarded Duncan? what not put upon
> His spongy officers, who shall bear the guilt
> Of our great quell?

(67–72)

These lines are the culmination of Lady Macbeth's appeal, and of her sexual rhetoric. "Perform" is the most obviously important of the chameleon words here. It alerts us to the continuing sense of the passage. But consider the five lines as a whole. The syntactic force of the impulse is active, transitive: the "spongy" officers are to receive what is put upon them, and "quell" becomes that which is achieved upon others. The syntax conduces to the half-realized metaphor which lies just beyond formulation here. The furniture, so to speak, of the unstated action is the bed. The words are *sleep, lie, perform upon, put upon, bear* (with its dual suggestion of "receive imprint" and "give birth to"). I put it: the tenor of the passage is sexual congress, and its final term, *great quell,* is the achievement of the act.

Our great quell. The commentaries, with their usual solidarity in the face of difficulties, offer a single gloss on *quell*: murder, killing, slaying. If it meant only that, Shakespeare might just as well have written "our great kill", which works perfectly well to accommodate the exigencies of scansion and editors. But Lady Macbeth's language is characterized by evasion or euphemism ("business", "enterprise", and so on), and "kill" is far too direct for her. *Quell* means something that "kill" does not. It is a curious word, used as a substantive by Shakespeare only in this passage. Its meaning must assimilate the verbal meanings of *quell,* and of the verb there is only a handful of instances in Shakespeare.[6] These instances comprehend *OED* sense 2: "To destroy, put an end to, suppress, extinguish, etc." and sense 3: "To crush or overcome (a person or a thing); to subdue, vanquish, reduce to subjection or submission; to force down to". The general meaning of "suppress", "subdue" is clearly permissible. But suppress what? The obvious associates are rebellion, insurrection, and so on. But Rabelais—in Urquhart's translation—thought that "Carnal concupiscence is cooled and quelled . . . by the means of wine".[7] Parallel, and even more striking, is a passage from Shakespeare himself:

> *Timon*   plague all:
> That your activity may defeat and quell
> The source of all erection.
>   (*Timon of Athens,* IV, iii, 162–4)

In each of these passages "quell" has the idea of suppressing (male) sexual potency. They do, I think, establish that the sexual tenor of Lady Macbeth's suasion endures to the final word. I add an outer but not remote possibility. The *OED* gives a rare sense of the verb *quell* (citing a 1340 usage) "To well out, flow" which is congruent with the argument here. It also relates well to the earlier "spongy". This other possibility reinforces but does not disturb the position. In sum: I hold that *quell* comprises the uppermost sense, "killing", and the underlying sense of "subdue sexual desire". Since the most direct way of subduing sexual desire is to yield to it, *quell* becomes a metaphor for killing the King. And in this, the word fits naturally, and climactically, into the sequence of terms that comprise the sexual underplot here.

The message is understood by Macbeth; he and his lady have no difficulty in comprehending the obliquities and nuances of their communication. "Bring forth men-children only" is his tribute, and at that moment it is much more than a simple recognition of her dauntlessness. A further question and answer, then comes Macbeth's decision. He delivers it in the mode in which their entire dialogue has been framed, and he assents, not so much to the argument, as to the metaphor:

> I am settled, and bend up
> Each corporal agent to this terrible feat.
>   (79–80)

"Bend up": howsoever the force of this metaphor is diffused over the body generally ("Each corporal agent"), its prime meaning originates from one agent only. At this play's heart of darkness, the killing of the King is conceived as phallic.

During this phase of the action, the play's language is saturated with the covert sexuality I have described. The opening lines of the following scene (II, i), the apparently normal dialogue between Banquo and Fleance, convey oddly sexual overtones. Thus:

Fleance   The moon is down; . . .
Banquo   And she goes down at twelve. . . .
            Hold, take my sword. There's husbandry in Heaven;

[cf. Lucio's pun on "husbandry", *Measure for Measure,* I, iv, 44,
and Sonnets XIII, 10 and III, 6]

            Their candles are all out.
                                (II, i, 2–5)

Is Shakespeare here implying a kind of oblique, glancing report on
Macbeth and his wife? At all events, the thematic ligature binding
the consecutive scenes, I, vii and II, i, is sexual. Macbeth, in his
following soliloquy, formalizes the matter. He identifies himself
with:

            wither'd murder,
    Alarum'd by his sentinel, the wolf
    Whose howl's his watch, thus with his stealthy pace,
    With Tarquin's ravishing strides, towards his design
    Moves like a ghost.
                                (II, i, 52–6)

"Tarquin's ravishing strides": the nature of the transaction receives
an open confirmation.

    And so to the second scene, and Lady Macbeth. Her opening
lines, uttered in a state of high excitement, would in a different
play-context (as, comedy of manners) pass easily as erotic:

    That which hath made them drunk hath made me bold;
    What hath quench'd them hath given me fire.
                                (II, ii, 1–2)

Lady Macbeth has taken wine with the two attendants. She has
now left Duncan's bedchamber, leaving her husband to commit the
murder. But the act is incomplete:

    And 'tis not done. Th' attempt and not the deed
    Confounds us.
                                (II, ii, 11–12)

"Deed": there is here the same terrible ambivalence that Middle-
ton knew, in: "Y'are the deed's creature".[8] The words she breathes
on Macbeth's return are of infinite significance: "My husband".
She never calls him this at any other time: it is at this moment
that their union is, by her, most fully acknowledged. Query or
recognition? The Folio gives a query after "My husband", while
modern editors allow her an exclamation. We need, in effect, both,
for the qualities of wonder, doubt, and recognition in her greeting.

And recognition is the theme of the question–answer passage that
follows. Consider the dark awareness of meaning, the precognition
vital to Shakespeare, in:

Macbeth	Who lies i'the second chamber?. . . .
Lady Macbeth	There are two lodged together.

(II, ii, 20, 26)

It is editorial officiousness to identify the "two lodged together" as
Malcolm and Donalbain, and not the two grooms. A literal meaning
does not arise readily from the passage at all. The only two who
matter are Macbeth and Lady Macbeth, "lodged together". It is
the meaning of the event *for them* that is the dominant fact of the
drama, and which impregnates their words. So, "sleep no more",
the thought which catches hold of Macbeth, is countered with Lady
Macbeth's:

> Why, worthy thane,
> You do unbend your noble strength, to think
> So brainsickly of things.

(II, ii, 44–6)

"Unbend" answers the "bend up / Each corporal agent" of I, vii:
the implied phallic image has a consistent narrative development,
for now the idea is of failure, of one "infirm of purpose", disturbed
by interruption and knockings. The close of II, ii (responding to the
opening of II, i) gives us terms that point again towards bed, this
time with wholly changed implications:

Lady Macbeth	retire we to our chamber. . . .
	Get on your nightgown, lest occasion call us,
	And show us to be watchers.

(II, ii, 66, 70–1)

But now the potential is stilled by circumstances and tone.

This point, as Shakespeare characteristically demonstrates, is made more clear in the ensuing scene, the Porter's. Now the play's sexuality moves out from the mental hinterland and assumes explicit form. Shakespeare's strategy, as so often, is to use his clowns to make plain that which was previously implicit. The "lechery" passage, then, fits easily with this strategy. But first, consider the symbolist implications of the setting. To the mass of commentary on the Porter's scene, I add that the dark room has a natural womb referent; and "turning the key", together with "knocking", are commonplace usage for sexual entry.[9] This is symbolist drama, and the scene's hell-references take over the senses of *hell* that Shakespeare explores in Sonnet CXLIV ("Two loves I have of comfort and despair"). The key line is "I guess one angel in another's hell" (1.12) and the best coverage is Stephen Booth's. His immediate gloss is "(1) each is a punishment for the other; they are one another's punishment; (2) one angel (the man) is in the other's (the woman's) hell".[10] Booth goes on to quote Ingram and Redpath on 1.12 :

> Several meanings appear to be present : (1) they are both in the 'Hell' or middle-den of a game of barley-break; (2) as contemporaries averred, such a position was often used as a pretext for a sexual tumble; (3) 'Hell' is probably also, as in Boccaccio's story of Rustico and Alibech (*Decameron*, III, 10), the female sexual organ.[11]

These associations, particularly (2) and (3), appear to me to bear directly upon *hell-gate*, the symbolist milieu for the Porter. The associations of sexuality (stemming from the female organ) and joint punishment for sin, are paramount.

In the play, the actual intruders turn out to be Macduff and Lennox; but in symbolic logic that is not the identity of the outside agent; he is clearly Macbeth, and I agree with Dowden's speculation that we "should ask whether Shakespeare did not make the porter use this word . . . with unconscious reference to Macbeth, who even then had begun to find that he could not 'equivocate to heaven.' "[12] "Equivocate" is Macbeth's word, and he, unmentioned, is at the back of everything the Porter says. The connection is carried forward into this sardonic account of the matter :

> *Porter*   Lechery, sir, it provokes, and unprovokes; it provokes
> desire, but takes away the performance : therefore, much
> drink may be said to be an equivocator with lechery :
> it makes him, and it mars him; it sets him on, and it
> takes him off; it persuades him, and disheartens him;
> makes him stand to and not stand to; in conclusion,
> equivocates him in a sleep, and, giving him the lie,
> leaves him.
>
> (II, iii, 32–40)

High tragedy becomes opera *buffo* for a moment, and there is here
a gross parody of the sexual impulse that has sustained Macbeth.
The idea is one of aspiration and failure; and this is the best single
version of Macbeth's activities throughout the play. But the Porter's
lines open out an additional vista, which the play's timing leaves
technically available. Does he, in effect, identify literally the failure
of Macbeth?

The language of this play speaks to us on several levels, and
moreover sexual action in *Macbeth* may be conceived of in different
ways. It may be thought of a a "pure" metaphor (desire for the
throne is akin to desire for anything else), or as an impulse that
flows around the margin of the possible, or as a literal fact, untrans-
lated. We shall not expect Shakespeare to close up his options for
us. His art is to multiply possibilities, to preserve the sense of life
constantly oscillating between metaphor and literal, between
analogue and the thing itself—and of a reality that embraces both.
I point out, then, that the Porter's address to Macduff and Lennox
has the force of a derisive epitome of Macbeth's relations with his
lady. In the logic of stage time, this is a possible, if in immediate
terms unlikely, outcome. The several minutes of Macbeth's absence
off-stage (though lengthened in stage dynamics by the slowness of
the Porter) scarcely furnish an ideal opportunity. And the
psychology of the moment, for both, is one of shock. But we have
to remember the nature of the invitation in Lady Macbeth's appeal
(I, vii, 67–72), and of the unstatable idea which, as it happens,
Shakespeare had stated explicitly at the beginning of his career. It
occurs in *Titus Andronicus*, that repository of information concerning the operations of the subconscious. Chiron and Demetrius,
having slain Bassianus, resolve to take his wife upon her dead
husband :

Chiron   Drag hence her husband to some secret hole,
          And make his dead trunk pillow to our lust.
                              (II, iii, 129–30)

I think it implausible that Shakespeare, in *Macbeth*, had forgotten what he knew during the writing of *Titus Andronicus*. But the main thrust of the Porter's epitome surely lies towards the future. There is a long-range failure of aspiration and act, and everything in the text tells us that it is located in the bed of the "two lodged together".

The play now moves into what, even so early, is in metaphor its latter phase. The idea of impotence and failure cannot be developed, only re-stated. Time and again the note of failure and doubt, often with a glancing sexual reference, is struck. There is an obvious hint in Banquo's:

> And when we have our naked frailties hid,
> That suffer in exposure . . .
>   (II, iii, 132–3)

and in Macbeth's response:

> Let's briefly put on manly readiness . . .
>   (II, iii, 139)

The definitive statement is given to Lady Macbeth, in soliloquy:

> Nought's had, all's spent,
> Where our desire is got without content:
>   (III, ii, 4–5)

"Spent" has, in Shakespeare, the senses of expenditure, loss and waste, and sexual discharge. Partridge gives for *spend* "to expend sexually", "to discharge seminally",[13] and his citation from *All's Well That Ends Well* is unarguable:

Parolles   He wears his honour in a box unseen,
            That hugs his kicky-wicky here at home,
            Spending his manly marrow in her arms . . .
                              (II, iii, 296–8)

It is if course reinforced by "The expense of spirit in a waste of shame". "Spent", then, joins "desire" and "content" in a grouping of chameleon-words.

There is, in the play's subliminal narrative, a certain resistance to the process of failure. Thus, in III, ii Lady Macbeth is still "love" (29), "dear wife" (36), "dearest chuck" (45). But this resistance diminishes. The motif of failure returns in III, iv (following the apparition of Banquo) and it emerges in these comments, all from Lady Macbeth:

> O, these flaws and starts . . . (63)

> What, quite unmann'd in folly? (73)

> Only it spoils the pleasure of the time. (98)

To this impression of twitching, pleasureless impotence may be added the caricature of abject weakness contained in Macbeth's "And push us from our stools" (82). "Stool", ludicrously, enlarges the hint in "purg'd" (75). The dialectic of weakness and resistance continues, but with a sense of ebbing powers; and the final words that Macbeth exchanges with his wife, on stage, contain the strangely imprecise hint of something lacking, that resolution cannot supply:

> *Macbeth*   Come, we'll to sleep. My strange and self-abuse
> Is the initiate fear that wants hard use;
> We are yet but young in deed.
>
> (III, iv, 142–4)

The sleepwalking scene (v, i) is the play's final statement concerning the sexual underplot. It is the terminal revelation of Lady Macbeth's mind, and in the play's design it is a kind of replay of II, i–ii, the murder scenes. The hallucinatory flux of impressions is not to be confined to a chronology or date, but the dominating mental context is clearly the night of the murder. Shakespeare, as Brian Vickers remarks, has "not only shown her perspective of time as being totally blurred, but has made her oscillations return always to the moments of severest guilt".[14] Even so, the indications are as fascinatingly imprecise as precise, and there is room for the imagination to roam over Lady Macbeth's words.

"Yet here's a spot" and "Out, damned spot" must be subsequent to the murder. But the next words indicate a point just before the murder: "One: two" (39) I take to be a precise time-reference, the sound of a clock. We have a fix on the murder, for Fleance and Banquo state that it is after twelve (ii, i, 1–3) and the Porter, roused by the same knocking which has disturbed Macbeth, says that "we were carousing till the second cock" (ii, iii, 25–6). *Romeo and Juliet* is unambiguous: "the second cock hath crow'd, / The curfew-bell hath rung, 'tis three o'clock" (iv, iv, 3–4). So the murder takes place around three o'clock, or shortly before. "One: two: why, then 'tis time to do't" (v, i, 39–40), Lady Macbeth's incitement to her husband may be addressed to him in their own bedchamber, or outside Duncan's. *When?* is the question her words generate, over and over. "No more o'that my Lord, no more o'that: you mar all with this starting" (48–50) insinuates a sexual context. The "starting" (cf. "flaws and starts", iii, iv, 63) suggests the sudden, nervous movements characteristic of Macbeth, which *mar* an activity together. And "mar" was the Porter's word: "it mars him" (ii, iii, 35). "Oh, oh, oh!" (58) is available in Shakespeare as an orgasmic sigh. In this sense, Colman allows as probable passages from *Troilus and Cressida* and *Cymbeline*.[15] The possibility can be plotted on the Shakespearean curve, from shadow towards the light: a moment later Lady Macbeth has "wash your hands, put on your nightgown; look not so pale" (69–70). This appears as a paraphrase of her Act ii injunctions:

> retire we to our chamber:
> A little water clears us of this deed: . . .
> Get on your nightgown, lest occasion call us,
> And show us to be watchers.
>
> (ii, ii, 66–70)

I point out that Lady Macbeth's later words refer as easily to the context of their own bedchamber, as the antechamber to Duncan's. And thus, Lady Macbeth's utterances from "No more o'that" to "look not so pale" form, or can be taken to form, a natural sequence.

The possibility of a time fix dissolves in her final:

> To bed, to bed! there's knocking at the gate: come come, come, give me your hand. What's done cannot be undone. To bed, to bed, to bed!
>
> (v, i, 73–6)

This must conflate her recollection of the murder with events since; as John Russell Brown remarks, she had not asked for his hand after the real murder.[16] The temporal and spatial imprecision of all this enfolds "to bed, to bed, to bed", a summons whose agonizing poignancy lies in the fact that it is divested of all erotic import. The unstated furniture of the I, vii, appeal has now become explicit; and in being acknowledged, it has lost all its meaning.

That is the play's last glimpse of Lady Macbeth, and what follows is in the nature of an epilogue. Macbeth's metaphors in Act v, to the extent that they are mildly sexual, all imply defeat. Thus, the "goose" and "lily-livered" images (v, iii, 11–15); "out, brief candle" (v, v, 23); "it hath cow'd my better part of man" (v, viii, 18). The *act* of I, vii achieves its final colouration in "a poor player / That struts and frets his hour upon the stage" (v, v, 24–5), thus indeed signifying that the earlier meanings of *act* have led to *nothing*. A course of action based upon a relationship has left Macbeth to face its terminal consequences, alone.

All this is, effectively, well understood on today's stage, where (as Carol Carlisle remarks) "the heavy modern emphasis is on the relationship between husband and wife", where "Lady Macbeth is a 'partner' rather than a tyrant".[17] Of late years, the best stage practice has depicted a strongly sexual bond between Macbeth and Lady Macbeth, most obviously in I, vii.[18] My concern here has been to examine the linguistic foundation of the drama : to explore the meaning of the act for Macbeth, and thus his relations with his wife. The stage directions are all in the words. Ultimately, they point towards the "dark, flowing current out of which surge the horrors, rhythmically and logically related", that Peter Brook discerned in an earlier play of Shakespeare's.[19] *Macbeth* then becomes a statement of sin and damnation, founded upon archetypal action of killing and sexuality. No other play of the mature Shakespeare reminds one so strongly that its author also wrote *Titus Andronicus*.

7 *Timon of Athens*

At the play's end, Alcibiades delivers this appraisal of the situation :

> Dead
> Is noble Timon : of whose memory
> Hereafter more. Bring me into your city,
> And I will use the olive with my sword,
> Make war breed peace, make peace stint war, make each
> Prescribe to other, as each other's leech.
> Let our drums strike.
>
> (v, iv, 79–85)

The word that resolves *Timon of Athens*—that interprets it—is "leech". Until overtaken by the sound of drums, its echoes hang over the play. What does *leech* mean? The major editions, with that unanimity that should always arouse one's suspicions, offer a terse footnote here : "*Leech,* physician". The commentary, as Housman remarked of Breiter's *Manilius,* is plain and concise, but meagre, and a student without other resource would starve on it.[1] The New Arden does indeed expand the gloss thus : "make each operate in such a way as to be for the good of the other, and so for the general good, as two physicians may prescribe for each other's ailments".[2] If we accept this, it makes the play's conclusion —and therefore, the play—an altogether blander affair than one had supposed. There is naturally another possibility. *Leech* can mean leech—the blood-sucking worm. Onions tells us that the original forms were distinct, but that in popular usage one was assimilated to the other.[3] In Shakespeare's day, both senses of "leech" were current. But the canon offers no clear guide to Shakespeare's usage. There is no other instance of "leech", if one excepts an early scene in *The Two Noble Kinsmen* where Palamon says :

> Let
> The blood of mine that's sib to him be suck'd
> From me with leeches!
>
> (I, ii, 71–3)[4]

Within the traditional canon, *leech* has to be defined by its context: a single play. I propose that its two major senses are contained within its sole occurrence; and that they correspond to the two divisions of *Timon of Athens*.

I

Timon is a bald instance of Shakespeare's two-part structures. And the great image of Part One is the feast. From his earliest work on, Shakespeare understood the potency and flexibility of feasting as stage symbol: thus the communal accord of *The Comedy of Errors*, the squabbling of *The Taming of the Shrew*, the shattered aspirations of *Macbeth*, the menace under the bonhomie of *Antony and Cleopatra*. In *Timon of Athens*, the two feasts focus the energies and meanings of the drama, from *Hautboys playing loud music* to "Uncover, dogs, and lap".

They do this, not merely in an open and explicit way, but because the two feasts are embedded in a running metaphoric commentary. It is *eat* (and *drink*) as metaphor that establishes the meaning of the spectacle. The terms come quickly to stand for human voracity, for people preying on Timon. Even the first appearance of the metaphor is ominous. The Poet imagines one "of Lord Timon's frame" whose followers "through him / Drink the free air" (I, i, 82–3), and who after spurn him. Then the metaphor is stated clearly:

Timon	Wilt dine with me, Apemantus?
Apemantus	No; I eat not lords.
Timon	An thou shouldst, thou'ldst anger ladies.
Apemantus	O, they eat lords; so they come by great bellies.

> (I, i, 206–10)

Eating is the figure for relationship. Alcibiades gives it a pleasantly ironic turn: he responds to Apemantus' curse with:

> Sir, you have sav'd my longing, and I feed
> Most hungerly on your sight.
>
> (I, i, 261–2)

The interplay between metaphor and literal is one of Shakespeare's most consistent resources, and there follows:

> *Second Lord*   Thou art going to Lord Timon's feast?
> *Apemantus*   Ay, to see meat fill knaves and wine heat fools . . .
> *First Lord*   Come, shall we in,
> And taste Lord Timon's bounty?
>
> (I, i, 270–2, 283–4)

The metaphor surfaces vividly in I, ii, and the proposition "that Timon is being devoured by his friends echoes through the Banquet of Sense which follows, and the Masque to feast the eyes. It is a triumph of the element of Air; music of the lutes contrasted with the more gloomy hautboys; airy dances, airy promises. . . ."[5] The commentary is supplied by Apemantus:

> I scorn thy meat; twould choke me, for I should ne'er flatter thee. O you gods, what a number of men eats Timon, and he sees 'em not! It grieves me to see so many dip their meat in one man's blood; and all the madness is, he cheers them up too.
>
> > I wonder men dare trust themselves with men:
> > Methinks they should invite them without knives;
> > Good for their meat, and safer for their lives.
>
> There's much example for't; the fellow that sits next him now, parts bread with him, pledges the breath of him in a divided draught, is the readiest man to kill him; 't has been proved. If I were a huge man, I should fear to drink at meals;
> Lest they should spy my windpipe's dangerous notes:
> Great men should drink with harness on their throats.
>
> (I, ii, 39–53)

Apemantus expounds the matter with didactic clarity. No record of performance exists, but Weimann has shown how the stage presentation of this passage would have pointed up its meaning. "Apemantus' stage position during the banquet scene . . . illustrates some of the potentialities of downstage acting on the Elizabethan platform stage. . . ." The banqueting table would probably be set up in the centre of the stage.

The men of elevated degree sit down at the main table in the middle of the stage, but at Timon's instruction, the grumbling Apemantus is given "a table by himself" downstage from the banquet table. The action that follows takes place, as the text indicates, on two levels: Timon and his guests delivering high-sounding speeches from the illusionistic area around the banqueting table (a true *locus*), Apemantus speaking usually in such a way that the audience, whom he faces, can hear, but those behind him cannot.[6]

The speech conventions are flexibly exploited here. The double shift prose–verse, prose–verse moves from a more informal, Timon-centred commentary to a generalizing, audience-directed address. Apemantus becomes a kind of stage lecturer, using metaphor to expound the meaning of the symbol.

The common metaphor multiplies individual discriminations. Alcibades and Timon discuss it :

> *Timon*   You had rather be at a breakfast of enemies than a dinner of friends.
>
> *Alcibiades* So they were bleeding-new, my lord, there's no meat like 'em : I could wish my best friend at such a feast.
>
> (i, ii, 78–82)

Eating people, for Alcibiades, is not wrong : he simply confines the practice to his enemies. Like Fortinbras, Alcibiades is presented not as an absolute model, but as the play's model, the necessary answer to the problems posed here. As for Apemantus, he repeats the point that Timon's guests are devouring him : "Thou weep'st to make them drink, Timon" (i, ii, 113). "We make ourselves fools, to disport ourselves; / And spend our flatteries, to drink those men / Upon whose age we void it up again . . ." (i, ii, 141–3). And Flavius, the honest steward, underlines the literal sense of the matter : Timon's household is "oppress'd / With riotous feeders" (ii, ii, 167–8). "How many prodigal bits have slaves and peasants / This night englutted!" (ii, ii, 174–5).

Apparently unchanged, the metaphor is already developing, for it points to surfeit and vomit. Now occurs the moment of decisive transformation, in Flaminius' scene end summary :

Let molten coin be thy damnation,
Thou disease of a friend, and not himself!
Has friendship such a faint and milky heart,
It turns in less than two nights? O you gods,
I feel my master's passion! this slave,
Unto his honour, has my lord's meat in him:
Why should it thrive and turn to nutriment,
When he is turn'd to poison?
O, may diseases only work upon't!
And, when he's sick to death, let not that part of nature
Which my lord paid for, be of any power
To expel sickness, but prolong his hour!

(III, i, 54–66)

This is a key phase in the underground narrative of *Timon*. Via the image of curdled milk, food is now converted to poison, and the idea of sickness begins to displace consumption. It is not a sharp change. Shakespeare goes to some trouble to keep the old idea going, introducing some choric Strangers to comment:

First Stranger   Who can call him
                    His friend that dips in the same dish?
                    . . . . he ne'er drinks,
                    But Timon's silver treads upon his lip . . .
                    . . . . For mine own part,
                    I never tasted Timon in my life.

(III, ii, 72–3, 77–8, 83–4)

This has the force of recapitulation. *Eating* expands into new metaphoric territory, that of *interest,* in:

Flavius   If money were as certain as your waiting,
            'Twere sure enough.
            Why then preferr'd you not your sums and bills,
            When your false masters eat of my lord's meat?
            Then they could smile and fawn upon his debts
            And take down th'interest into their glutt'nous maws.

(III, iv, 46–52)

This move enables *interest* to link up with *sickness,* too, for Timon's response to his creditors' bills is:

Timon	Knock me down with 'em: cleave me to the girdle.
Lucius' Servant	Alas, my lord—
Timon	Cut my heart in sums.
Titus	Mine, fifty talents.
Timon	Tell out my blood.
Lucius' Servant	Five thousand crowns, my lord.
Timon	Five thousand drops pays that.

(III, iv, 91–7)

The collocation is eating/usury/blood-letting. And it is repeated. The hysteria of Timon is matched by the harder, controlled rage of Alcibiades:

Banish me !

> Banish your dotage; banish usury,
> That makes the senate ugly.

(III, v, 98–100)

and

> I'm worse than mad: I have kept back their foes,
> While they have told their money and let out
> Their coin upon large interest, I myself
> Rich only in large hurts. All those for this?
> Is this the balsam that the usuring senate
> Pours into captains' wounds?

(III, v, 106–11)

The devourers of Timon are those of the community also.

The banquet of III, vi, focuses and develops the ideas presented so far. The feast, in name and form only, is introduced with a tight satiric scorn that recalls Jonson (as does much else in this play): "Each man to his stool . . . [with the obvious implication], with that spur as he would to the lip of his mistress: your diet shall be in all places alike. Make not a City feast of it, to let the meat cool ere we can agree upon the first place: sit, sit" (III, vi, 73–7), which glancingly hits at the City banquets of Shakespeare's day. Athens is a city much like London. The magnates of the City appear clearly enough in :

The gods require our thanks.
You great benefactors, sprinkle our society with thankfulness.
For your own gifts, make yourselves praised : but reserve still
to give, lest your deities be despised. Lend to each man enough,
that one need not lend to another; for, were your godheads
to borrow of men, men would forsake the gods.

(III, vi, 77–83)

"Gods" is converted with anagrammatic ease to "dogs",[7] and "Uncover, dogs, and lap" (III, vi, 95). What is it that they lap?

The dishes, discreetly described in the stage directions of modern editions as *full of warm water,* present the antithesis and yet the logical continuation of the first banquet. The element of air has now become "smoke" (99), hence the link with "mouth-friends" (99), "last" [breath] (100), and "vapours" (107). "Smoke", let us note, has somewhat changed its meaning today. *The Concise Oxford Dictionary* (sixth edition) defines it as "Visible volatile products of burning". For the Elizabethans, smoke meant not only "sooty exhalations"[8] (and as such, something distinctly disagreeable), but vapours. Again, the sense was usually adverse : thus "O night, thou furnace of foul-reeking smoke" (*Rape of Lucrece,* I, 799), and the clouds' "rottten smoke" (Sonnet XXXIV, 4). In Timon's charge, "smoke" becomes a figure for "empty talk", but the literal from which the figure emerges means "foul vapour" and not (as one would infer from a modern stage direction) "steam" (with its cleansing, hospital associations). The nature of the dishes' liquid contents is unmistakably indicated. "Each man to his *stool"* leads to *"sprinkle* our society with thankfulness". It is the revenge of Timon "Who, *stuck* and *spangled* with your flatteries [i.e. bespattered and decorated], / Washes it off, and *sprinkles* in your faces / Your *reeking* villainy (101–3). Hence the attraction of this noisome fluid for "time's flies" (106), and their known association with "vapours" (107). (Cf. Hamlet's "foul and pestilential congregation of vapours", II, ii, 313–14.) These tainted puddles are what the City dogs are invited to lap.

Once the import of this passage is understood, the curse which concludes it appears not simply as a rhetorical climax, but an organically logical outcome :

> Of man and beast the infinite malady
> Crust you quite o'er ! What, dost thou go ?

> Soft! take thy physic first—thou too—and thou;
> Stay, I will lend thee money, borrow none.
>
> (III, vi, 108–11)

Nothing but plague can come from such filth, and this "physic", homeopathically, is the only cure for Athens. The scatological motif, latent in "money" here (the implications I shall consider later), surfaces again a moment later with Timon's jeering "What, all in motion?" (112). (Cf. "he gives me the potions and the motions", *The Merry Wives of Windsor,* III, i, 104–5.) His exit concludes Part One, and Part Two explores the now established metaphoric situation, the plague.

II

The energy, the animating impulse of Part Two is the curse. It is focused to a word, "plague", which unites the senses of anathema and pestilent disease. These senses hold different dramatic significances. *Plague* as curse is a vehement impulse, a muscular form of stage expressionism. It does not lend itself to analysis, and its unvarying monotone is, on stage, the play's chief problem. *Plague* as disease contains an intellectual analysis, a metaphoric perception. Timon takes disease as the figure for the human condition, and moreover holds the literal state of disease to be its only cure. So Timon's final "four words" (I follow the Folio here, though "sour" is tempting) are "Plague and infection mend [what is amiss]," and they constitute his motto-statement.

It is unnecessary to muster up card-index legions of disease images. The most casual of readers could pass an examination on the iterative theme here. "Plagues, incident to men" is the designed centre of Timon's first Misanthropos tirade (IV, i, 21), and it generates an immediate catalogue of ills, ranging from "sciatica" (probably syphilis), through itches, blains, and leprosy. Such ills, with variations, recur steadily throughout the remainder of the play. The primary verb of transmission is *infect*: hence "Breath infect breath, / That their society, as their friendship, may / Be merely poison (IV, i, 30–2). "Breath" is the development of Part One's "air". Society is to punish itself with its own corrupt mouthings. More, the sun itself is to aid the course of pestilence:

> O blessed breeding sun, draw from the earth
> Rotten humidity; below thy sister's orb
> Infect the air!
>
> (IV, iii, 1–3)

"Rotten humidity" is an intensification of the feast's "smoke". One receives the impression of a contextual metaphor akin to a swamp or fen—steamy, rotting, plague-breeding.

Such a metaphor is congruent with both main streams of disease that are alluded to. Shakespeare may not have made our distinction between "infectious" and "contagious", but those ills which are incurred by touch are included in his catalogue, most notably leprosy and syphilis. Syphilis is the major contact disease here, and it dramatizes the mechanisms of action and reaction. There is a deal of reference to it in Act IV, much of it centring on the two whores. These have, in Timon's mind, the role of infecting mankind more rapidly, of stimulating society to circulate its diseases. The symbol and agent of the whores' trade is gold, the "common whore of mankind" (IV, iii, 42). Gold, for a space, is what this play preoccupies itself with. It requires separate discussion. What is gold in *Timon of Athens*?

"Gold", in *Timon*, has already had a certain controversy. Wilson Knight considered it a major image motif.[9] Yet Caroline Spurgeon pointed out that although "gold" is spoken of twenty times in Act IV, "there is only one image from gold throughout the play".[10] For her, the chain of images associated with dogs was more important. Technically, the standing of "gold" appears as literal reference, heavily emphasized, and meaning no more and no less than "money". The main question is whether gold (money) is the true subject of discussion, or a mutation and index of Timon's loathing of mankind.

Marx took the first view, and in his single contribution to Shakespeare criticism cited Timon's:

> Gold? Yellow, glittering, precious, gold? No, Gods,
> I am no idle votarist! . . .
> Thus much of this will make black white, foul fair,
> Wrong right, base noble, old young, coward valiant.
> . . . Why, this
> Will lug your priests and servants from your sides,

> Pluck stout men's pillows from below their heads :
> This yellow slave
> Will knit and break religions, bless the accursed;
> Make the hoar leprosy adored, place thieves
> And give them title, knee, and approbation
> With senators on the bench : This it is
> That makes the wappen'd widow wed again;
> She, whom the spital-house and ulcerous sores
> Would cast the gorge at, this embalms and spices
> To the April day again. Come, damned earth,
> Thou common whore of mankind, that putt'st odds
> Among the rout of nations.
>
> (IV, iii, 26–43)[11]

After quoting this, and "O thou sweet king-killer", etc. (IV, iii, 382–93), Marx comments : "Shakespeare excellently depicts the real nature of *money.*" Following a passage dealing with Goethe, comes this :

Shakespeare stresses especially two properties of money : (1) It is the visible divinity—the transformation of all human and natural properties into their contraries, the universal confounding and overturning of things : it makes brothers of impossibilities. (2) It is the common whore, the common pimp of people and nations.

The overturning and confounding of all human and natural qualities, the fraternization of impossibilities—the *divine* power of money—lies in its *character* as men's estranged, alienating and self-disposing *species nature.* Money is the alienated *ability of mankind.*[12]

Marx, disarmingly, turns out to be a Marxist commentator, though not a vulgar Marxist. Since his true subject is money, not *Timon,* it is scarcely fair to press an adverse commentary on him here. Still, the passage is sometimes cited as an illumination of the text,[13] and a few comments are in order. First, the play's statement is not co-extensive with Timon's statement (in two major speeches). This caution applies to all commentators who abstract a single major passage, and found on it an exegetical edifice. "Shakespeare excellently depicts", then, Timon's *perception* of "the real nature of money". Next, Marx's argument can be stood on its head. If, as he says, "Money . . . appears as this *overturning* power both against the individual and against the bonds of society, etc., which claim to be essences in themselves",[14] it can as easily be asserted that money is the social bond that unites a community. "Money is the alienated *ability of mankind*. That which I am unable to do as a *man,* and of which therefore all my individual essential powers are incapable, I am able to do by means of *money*." Apply this to Timon, and money appears as the bond which linked him to Athenian society. Timon, rich, is potentially alienated: Timon, poor, is actually so. He becomes alienated *because* he lacks the ability of money; his "individual essential powers" were expressed above all in the giving away of money. Moreover, money fails to transform everyone in *Timon*. Alcibiades remains a courteous and loyal friend, ready to share his limited gold with Timon. Flavius remains a faithful servant. Their "individual essential powers" are expressed through, as well as against, money. As for the "common whore of mankind", the metaphor is actualized in the flesh of Timandra and Phrynia. It is perfectly arguable, through the name-echo, that "Timandra" is a face of Timon, his "semblable"; one whore denounces another. I add that *Timon of Athens* does not present a case against whores. It merely establishes that the Timon of Part Two does not like them, especially when they happen to be called Timandra. The entry of Alcibiades with a brace of whores (presumably, one on each arm) makes its own emblematic point: society is inevitably disposed to make use of these human resources. Alcibiades, with his unfailing courtesy and tempered generosity, suggests a perspective on "whores" that is as superior as it is opposed to Timon's.[15]

Shakespeare, in "stressing the two properties of money", is in fact depicting human nature by means of its attitude towards money. Timon's self-hatred stems from his past relations with gold. As Empson remarks, "This is a refinement of money hatred that Marx failed to pick out of the play; Timon's generosity was a way of begging for affection, and it makes him the same kind of dog as the spaniels he could hire".[16] One can scarcely take Timon as an objective analyst of gold's effect, and the play does not go on to support him.

For similar reasons, I think it an error of interpretation to take "gold" in *Timon* as the centrepiece of a serious social commentary, as for instance E. C. Pettet does.[17] In such an approach, one assumes that the play is "about" usury, and that its prime meaning is disclosed in IV, iii. It appears to me that gold in this instance reveals Timon's subjectivity. It is a means through which Timon recognizes the world, and himself; gold for him is a figure and agent of the corruption in human relations. No monetary reform would change the nature of those relations. Naturally, Shakespeare conducts his audience through a phase in which allusion is made to the contemporary social abuses of London. That is a factor of audience reaction, but it does not identify the core of the play. I add that there is a needless naiveté in taking the theme of *Timon* as "the wickedness of usury",[18] as though *usury* were a simple, bad word on whose meaning all (save moneylenders) could agree. "Usury" was a complex term, a debate word. By the time of *Timon* "usury" had already begun to acquire the tension, which the *OED* demonstrates as a confirmed tendency of its usage, between two major senses: the taking of interest, and the taking of excessive interest. And the moral argument over sense one (the taking of interest) was rapidly retreating into antiquity. Whatever the date of *Timon*, it very probably came after Bacon's 1606 collection of essays. In it, his highly sophisticated treatment takes "usury" for granted:

> . . . it is a vanity to conceive that there would be ordinary borrowing without profit; and it is impossible to conceive the number of inconveniences that will ensue, if borrowing be cramped. Therefore to speak of the abolishing of usury is idle. All states have ever had it, in one kind or rate or other. So as that opinion must be sent to Utopia.[19]

"Usury", for Bacon, is obviously necessary, and the problem is primarily one of regulation, for preference through a two-tier rate system. Alcibiades does indeed identify the "large interest" of the Athenian senators (III, v, 108), and to that extent Shakespeare fixes a type of social abuse. But that is not to allow the entire play as a diatribe against the taking of interest.

What, then, is "gold" in *Timon of Athens*? Up to a point, one can agree with Winifred Nowottny's view of it: "Timon's gold is not so much a prime and perfected symbol as a maker of collateral symbols".[20] Certainly gold, as it appears in Act IV, governs a phase in the imagistic transformations of the drama. It is associated with earth, roots, even food: "Earth, yield me roots! / Who seeks for better of thee, sauce his palate / With thy most operant poison! / What is here? / Gold?" (IV, iii, 23–6). It then becomes "This yellow slave", "Thou common whore of mankind", and thus introduces Timandra and Phrynia. Its immediate function as a linking agent is clear. And yet, there is a larger symbolic association that is always at the back of the action, in the play's imaginative hinterland.

"Money is like muck", said Bacon, "not good except it be spread".[21] The association between gold and dung must be as old as the language, perhaps as old as social man. Shakespeare's contemporaries knew it well enough. One need look no further than the *Oxford Dictionary of English Proverbs*.[22] "Gold is but the earths garbadge" is Lyly, in *Midas* (1592), ii, ii, 5. "Yron and golde which are earths excrements" stated Nashe, in *Terrors of Night* (1594), i, 352. Jonson one would expect to add to this section of the lexicon of proverbial lore, and does: "Gold is but muck" comes from *The Case is Altered* (1609), iv, ix, 20. The action of this latter play extends considerably the curt quotation. One of the *dramatis personae*, subtly named Jacques de Prie, enters (iii, v) *with his gold and a scuttle full of horsedung*. "Ile hide and cover it with this horsedung: / Who will suppose that such a precious nest / Is crownd with such a dunghill excrement?"[23] He does this, and the loss (false, then real) of the gold furnishes much of the fun in Acts iv and v. Jonson makes his points graphically and energetically, with a tireless faith in their capacity to delight and elevate. We can draw the easy conclusion, that Shakespeare and his contemporaries were sufficiently acquainted with the symbolic linking of gold and muck.

And we need that association to understand *Timon*. There is an undeniable air of the privy about the play, created by many "secret impressions" (in Morgann's phrase),[24] and explicit in certain terms. Some of this effect can be assigned to the second feast, which, as I have argued, generates a strong sense of communal corruption. Some of it can be discerned in that stratum of the play's language that, innocent as it seems, is energized—or infected —by the more forceful passages. Let us begin with "flow": an unsurprising word, yet one-fifth of its occurrences in Shakespeare are in *Timon*, which suggests a special importance. An acid dialogue between Second Lord and Apemantus registers the "flow" of Timon's health (i, ii, 56–60) and Flavius identifies the "flow of riot" (ii, ii, 3). Flavius continues with "I have retir'd me to a wasteful cock, / And set mine eyes at flow" (ii, ii, 171–2). The subliminal proposition is that Timon's generosity is an outflow:

> *Senator*   Still in motion
>   Of raging waste? It cannot hold; it will not.
>   (II, i, 3–4)

That proposition would be affirmed, to an Elizabethan, by Apemantus' later action in offering Timon a medlar. At one level, this episode is simply an opportunity for (rather obvious) word play on "meddle". Underneath is the use of medlar. The *OED* cites Elyot (1533) as noting that "Medlars ar cold and dry, and constrictife." Gerard, in his *Herball,* lays it down as the first of its virtues: "Medlars do stop the belly especially when they be greene and harde; for after that they have been kept a while, so that they become soft and tender, they do not binde or stop so much, but are the more fit to be eaten".[25] The usual sexual senses of "medlar"—as in *Romeo and Juliet, Measure for Measure*—are absent here. But then, this is a play virtually devoid of sexual undertones.[26] Apemantus, as I interpret the passage, is offering a precise and pointed physic for Timon's complaint.

The general contours of Timon's condition, physical and mental, are suggested by a cluster of terms, which quicken in Act IV. "Flow" leads to other hints of liquid waste: Timon calls on the Athenian youth to debauch itself, "That 'gainst the stream of virtue they may strive, / And drown themselves in riot" (IV, i, 27–8). (Compare Alcibiades' promise that his soldiers will not "offend the stream / Of regular justice", v, iv, 60–1.) "Drown" leads to Timon's recommendation to the Poet and Painter, "Hang them or stab them, drown them in a draught" (v, i, 105), *draught* being a cesspool or sink. Timon refers to the "common wrack" of Athens (v, i, 195), and H. J. Oliver has drawn attention to the fact that *wrack* can mean "the rubbish washed down or deposited by moving water".[27] The *OED* is suggestive here, and sense 3b seems especially apposite: "Weeds, rubbish, waste etc. floating on, or washed down or ashore by, a river, pond, or the like." Another citation indicates that farmers used wrack for manure. Anything the Painter says is eaten up by its own satire, and his remark that the Poet and himself "Have travail'd in the great *show'r* of your gifts" (v, i, 73) requires no gloss. *Shower* (which recalls the earlier sprinkle) adds point to the final word in Timon's closing "Sun, hide thy beams! Timon hath done his *reign*" (v, i, 226). The Folio spelling here, a little oddly, is "Raigne". The usual spelling for "reign" is "reigne", just as the usual spelling for "rain" is "raine". It is as though the compositor conflated the two spellings "reigne" and "raine" in his mind—or that Shakespeare did.[28] I take Timon's last word as word play: his statement is that he has done railing, and raining, on the world.

These hints cluster around the central association. To them we ought to add *heap,* a word open to inflection and context. (Cf. Richard's scornful "Among this princely *heap*", *Richard III,* II, i, 53; and Henry's "For this they have engross'd and pil'd up / The cank'red *heaps* of strange achieved gold"; *2 Henry IV,* IV, v, 71–2, itself a link with the money/muck association.) In this play, the bandits' reference to Timon's "mass of treasure" (IV, iii, 405) broadens into the Senators' promise of *"heaps* and sums of love and wealth" (v, i, 155); the word is coloured by Alcibiades' "When I have laid proud Athens on a *heap*" (IV, iii, 101), which suggests that he will throw Athens on a dunghill. All leads to the passage where Shakespeare makes his most explicit *verbal* statement of the idea, Timon's speech linking gold and cosmic thievery; and it comes down to this: "the earth's a thief, / That feeds and breeds by a composture stol'n / From gen'ral excrement:" (IV, iii, 443–5). Those are the words, what is left is the action: and the Folio provides no stage direction to point the meaning of Timon's outburst to Painter and Poet: "You are an alchemist; make gold of *that!"* (v, i, 117). The symbolic standing of *gold* in this play is, by now, sufficiently established; and the nature of what Timon thrusts at his visitors is not hard to divine. Peter Brook, to my mind, drew the correct deduction from the text, in his production of *Timon d'Athènes* at the Bouffes-du-Nord (1974): and his Timon hurled, at the flatterers, excrement.

Eating, disease, the ordure that is money: these are the elements that dominate the second half of *Timon.* They compose a harsh, schematic diagram of human existence in which the mechanisms of sex are absorbed into the teleology of disease. Part Two becomes an intensified desperate replay of Part One, with the same cast enacting a drama of primal horror in Timon's mind. The "Amazons" become Timandra and Phrynia; the Poet and Painter return, "Having often of your open bounty tasted" (v, l, 61); the courtesy of Alcibiades and the bitterness of Apemantus are equally unendurable, because they knew him before; the "friends" became banditti. The motifs return too. The figure of eating moves from Timon's appeal to the banditti:

> Your greatest want is, you want much of meat.
> Why should you want? Behold, the earth hath roots;
> Within this mile break forth a hundred springs;
> The oaks bear mast, the briers scarlet hips;
> The bounteous housewife, nature, on each bush
> Lays her full mess before you. Want! why want?
>
> (IV, iii, 419–24)

to his recognition, "You must eat men" (428). Timon, who has eaten the world, "Who had the world as my confectionery" (IV, iii, 260),[29] wills the refinements of feasting upon the banditti, as the shortest route to terminal fever:

> Here's gold. Go, suck the subtle blood o'the grape,
> Till the high fever seeth your blood to froth,
> And so 'scape hanging: trust not the physician . . .
>
> (IV, iii, 432–4)

Note the collocation of *blood-sucking* and *physician,* two lines apart, which are to fuse in the final *leech.* Disease and brute appetite now obsess Timon, and the Act IV synthesis comes in "And may diseases lick up their false bloods!" (IV, iii, 539). Timon's vision, however subject to external judgment ("This is in thee a nature but infected" says Apemantus, IV, iii, 202), structures the later stages of the play. The vision is not at odds with Timon's own diagnosis: "my long sickness / Of health and living now begins to mend . . ." (V, i, 189–90).

The metaphor of disease does not terminate with Timon. He bequeaths it to the play. And he announces that ominous reciprocity of disease and treatment that is to resolve the play: "Be Alcibiades your plague, you his" (V, i, 192). Alcibiades, whether speaking or silent, dominates the final scene. He proclaims the revolution that health and youth force upon corruption and age:

> now the time is flush,
> When crouching marrow in the bearer strong
> Cries of itself 'No more:' now breathless wrong
> Shall sit and pant in your great chairs of ease,
> And pursy insolence shall break his wind
> With fear and horrid flight.
>
> (V, iv, 8–13)

The hints of gross corruption are at one with the air of this play. "Noble and young", the Senators' term of address, appears as the principle of regeneration, the answer to the general mythic picture of infertility and death. The Senators now, speaking in turn, develop this principle of regeneration into a programme of punishment and reform. Alcibiades listens as they vary the figure of physician, and seek to fasten the role upon him :

> We sent to thee, to give thy rages balm . . .
>
> (16)

> By decimation, and a tithed death—
> If thy revenges hunger for that food
> Which nature loathes—take thou the destin'd tenth,
> And by the hazard of the spotted die
> Let die the spotted.
>
> (31–5)

> like a shepherd,
> Approach the fold and cull th'infected forth,
> But kill not all together.
>
> (42–4)

Alcibiades accepts the role, and his final words carry the unchallengeable dual authority of soldier and physician. "Noble", the word attached to Timon in Part One, now rests upon Alcibiades, though—typically—he does not withhold it from his friend, "Dead / Is noble Timon" (80). His response to the Senators carries with it the hint of purification as well as purgation, the promise that corruption shall go no further :

> and, to atone your fears
> With my more noble meaning, not a man
> Shall pass his quarter, or offend the stream
> Of regular justice in your city's bounds . . .
>
> (58–61)

It is a promise symbolically realized in Timon's final state, "entomb'd upon the very hem o'th'sea" (65). The soldier–reporter confirms Timon's last words :

> Timon hath made his everlasting mansion
> Upon the beached verge of the salt flood;
> Who once a day with his embossed froth
> The turbulent surge shall cover:
>
> (v, i, 218–21)

Mansion: it is a glancing reference to the mediaeval idea of the body as a "house of corruption". Daily the ocean will cleanse it. Alcibiades offers his own interpretation:

> Though thou abhorr'dst in us our human griefs,
> Scorn'dst our brain's flow and those our droplets which
> From niggard nature fall, yet rich conceit
> Taught thee to make vast Neptune weep for aye
> On thy low grave, on faults forgiven.
>
> (v, iv, 75–9)

And then Alcibiades issues his order, announces his intentions, and draws the conclusion of the drama:

> Bring me into your city,
> And I will use the olive with my sword,
> Make war breed peace, make peace stint war, make each
> Prescribe to other as each other's leech.
>
> (81–4)

Three propositions are contained in the final lines:

(1) peace and war will prescribe to each other, like physicians, for the common good;
(2) peace and war (perhaps, citizen and soldier) will fasten upon each other, like bloodsuckers;
(3) the first and second propositions are simultaneously true. Peace and war are not exclusive states, but reactivating impulses in the symbiosis of social existence.

This third proposition is, effectively, what the servants agree upon, in their *Coriolanus* dialogue:[30]

> *Second Servant*   and as war, in some sort, may be said to be a
> ravisher, so it cannot be denied but peace is a
> great maker of cuckolds.

<table>
<tr><td>First Servant</td><td>Ay, and it makes men hate one another.</td></tr>
<tr><td>Third Servant</td><td>Reason, because they then less need one another. The wars for my money.</td></tr>
</table>

(IV, iv, 242–7)

Alcibiades confirms, more bleakly, the analysis of the leading political thinkers in *Coriolanus*. The mutuality of war and peace, the continuing tension of blood-letting and blood-sucking, is his theme. The Athenian society that devoured Timon must submit to the physic of decimation. Thus *leech* is the remedy, as much as the analysis, of the Athenian corruption; and Alcibiades, in the end, is the only man who has the right to interpret the action : the corruption that is Athens yields only to the man "That does both act and know". It is, after all, the same Athens for Timon and Alcibiades. One offers a passion of invective, the other a disciplined, and discriminating, exercise of the controls of blood-letting. *This*, the play proposes, is the only cure for *that*. The final position—proposition 3, as I take it—is the more terrible for the elegant severity of the demonstration, focused as it is to a terminal word play. *Timon* looks like the supreme statement of the black Shakespeare, and it is blacker than it looks.

8 *The Winter's Tale:* A Dance to the Music of Time

The formal principle of *The Winter's Tale,* clearly, is best identified as time. There is no single or dominant way of defining time, an immensely complex notion; and Turner, in his study of time in Shakespeare, finds nine major aspects.[1] They lend themselves to diverse critical approaches. If, for instance, we take our cue from Time as Chorus, the physical presence of Time in Act IV brings with him the iconographic traditions of Time the revealer and Time the destroyer.[2] The play's organization into two parts invites a structural analysis based on parallel.[3] Since *The Winter's Tale* is the most clear-cut instance of Shakespeare's two-part structures, the sixteen-year gap asserts the literal fact of time's passage. David Young has detected the different pacing, hence the different concepts of time, in the first and second half: "the first, linear, impetuous, irrevocable, enemy to human aspirations; the second, cyclic, leisurely, restorative, in harmony with man's hopes".[4] The spacious and leisurely fourth Act brings with it a new dimension to time, and invests with deep meaning the play's imagery of seasonal growth and change. Through it, the associated ideas of regeneration and salvation are easily discoverable. All these possibilities are glosses on time as change, and for the most part stay close to the word "time". One cannot, however, analyse this play through a single word. I want to explore here some other ways in which Shakespeare apprehends time, and to pursue the concept into the realms of metaphor and comic theory. This play evolves through the structuring metaphors of wave and dance, and ultimately presents laughter as the challenge to time.

I

The basic way in which one conceives of time is a linear progress, an unimpeded advance towards an unreached future. In the crudest way, this corresponds to the forward narrative movement of most dramatic designs, to which *The Winter's Tale* is no exception. But the direct forward movement is Shakespeare's plan in only the most shallow sense. He works from a series of strong dramatic impulses that proceed past–future, past–future. Some early instances: I, i ("If you shall chance, Camillo, to visit Bohemia") is based on future/present/future alternating impulses. Scene ii moves from the recent past ("Nine changes of the wat'ry star hath been / The shepherd's note since we have left our throne") to the near future of departure, then from the remoter past (the boyhood of Polixenes and Leontes) to the present: "Looking on the lines / Of my boy's, face, methoughts I did recoil / Twenty-three years, and saw myself unbreech'd" (153–5). The scene ends with the approaching future of Polixenes' flight, "Come, sir, away". Leontes' hallucinations move between the recent past, and the coming decision of the oracle; Paulina's plan is for the future ("He must be told on't", II, ii, 31); Cleomenes and Dion report the past of their mission (III, i), which translates into the guarded prophecy of the oracle. The technique continues till the very end, when the total play becomes a springboard into the future: "hastily lead away". Thus the aftermath of the play becomes a kind of courtship, mirroring the reported courtship of I, ii, "Three crabbed months had sour'd themselves to death" (102). So far from moving forward in an undeviating line, the energies of the play constantly shuttle from past to future, from the present to its references in time. Indeed, the living present—so Shakespeare postulates—can only exist in relation to past and future.

This sense of the living present is captured above all in IV, iv, which criticism unites in taking to be central to the play's experience. The richly varied flowers express Shakespeare's concept here, as they move forth and back in the natural cycle of time. In detail:

(1)   IV, iii, is in mood the prologue to the great IV, iv scene. It opens with Autolycus' song, which appears to set the scene with precision:

> When daffodils begin to peer,
> With heigh! the doxy over the dale,
> Why, then comes in the sweet o'th' year;
> For the red blood reigns in the winter's pale.

Daffodils, in the south of England, appear in March; sometimes they are seen by March 1st. Gerard, in his *Herball*, allows that it "flowreth in the month of Aprill, and sometimes sooner".[5] Even if we allow for the slightly harsher winters of Shakespeare's era, and the consequent retarding of the daffodil's appearance, he clearly thinks of it as a March flower (as in IV, iv, 120). There is an easy assumption that Autolycus is singing *in*, as well as *of*, March. But the third verse of his song runs :

> The lark, that tirra-lyra chants,
> With heigh ! with heigh ! the thrush and the jay,
> Are summer songs for me and my aunts,
> While we lie tumbling in the hay.

After the transition of the undatable second verse, Autolycus looks forward to high summer—or sings from within it. So there is a time-movement within his song, spring/summer.

(2)   After his song, Autolycus encounters the Clown, on his way to make purchases for the sheep-shearing feast. Now this feast was always a midsummer affair,[6] and since the feast in the framework of IV, iv we have to view it as the central dating element. The suggestion, however, is of the passage of time, since the entire movement takes Autolycus' opening line as its point of departure.

(3)   The same artful transition occurs at the beginning of IV, iv. We now have the feast proper, which is presumed to follow the Clown's errand. Yet Florizel's initial address to Perdita mentions, and apparently fixes the time at, April :

> These your unusual weeds to each part of you
> Do give a life : no shepherdess, but Flora
> Peering in April's front. This your sheep-shearing
> Is as a meeting of the petty gods,
> And you the queen on't.
>
> (1–5)

The immediate suggestion is that Perdita is decked in the flowers of **April**. This is strictly impossible : April flowers do not survive to midsummer. What is important is the force of suggestion, the idea that Perdita/Flora is an emblem of spring—even in midsummer. She becomes a fusion of spring and summer.

(4)   Perdita offers flowers to Polixenes and Camillo:

> Reverend sirs,
> For you, there's rosemary and rue; these keep
> Seeming and savour all the winter long:
> Grace and remembrance be to you both,
> And welcome to our shearing!
>
> (73–7)

Polixenes admits ruefully the decorum: "well you fit our ages / With flow'rs of winter" (78–9). Gerard notes: "Rosemarie flowreth twise a yeere, in the spring, and after in August. The wilde Rosemarie flowreth in Iune and Iulie".[7] As for rue, "They flower in these colde countries in Iuly and August; in other countries sooner".[8] Thus the symbolism points to winter, while the actuality stands at midsummer.

(5)   Again:

> *Perdita*   Sir, the year growing ancient,
> Not yet on summer's death, nor on the birth
> Of trembling winter, the fairest flow'rs o'th' season
> Are our carnations and streak'd gillyvors . . .
>
> (79–82)

The syntax is most artful. The present participle, "the year growing ancient", implies that the season of the statement was late summer. It is easy to read the passage casually in that sense. No such commitment is made, since Perdita means *"when the year grows ancient ..."* So:

(6)   Perdita reifies the literal, natural present of the scene with

> Here's flow'rs for you;
> Hot lavender, mints, savory, marjoram;
> The marigold, that goes to bed wi' th' sun
> And with him rises weeping: these are flow'rs
> Of middle summer, and I think they are given
> To men of middle age.
>
> (103–8)

It is a courtly adjustment of decorum, and symbol and literal now fuse.

(7) Finally, Perdita calls for the flowers of spring—already past—for Florizel. "Now, my fair'st friend, / I would I had some flow'rs o'th' spring that might / Become your time of day", and the great catalogue of daffodils, primroses, and the rest of the spring flowers, follows (112–27). Just as the movement opened with spring looking forward to summer, it closes with summer looking back—or forward—to spring.

IV, iii and IV, iv, then, compose a set-piece in which, with immense virtuosity, Shakespeare executes variations on the time-motif. Based on the literal present of midsummer, the sheep-shearing scene constantly deploys flowers to look forwards and back. This rhythmic movement in time is best described as a wave.

II

Wave: we apprehend here a ridge-like cross-section, one of a series marked by a rising and falling motion. It is both a defined shape in itself, and a unit in a series constantly in motion. Physically, the wave is realized in the movement of the sea, and Shakespeare had already caught the process in Sonnet LX:

> Like as the waves make towards the pebbled shore,
> So do our minutes hasten to their end;
> Each changing place with that which goes before,
> In sequent toil all forwards do contend.[9]

"Wave" is in Shakespeare the metaphor for rhythmic movement, and thus the principle of life itself. The importance of "wave" to *The Winter's Tale* was recognized long ago. Caroline Spurgeon made the connection with Sir James Jeans, quoting with approval his *The Mysterious Universe*: "The tendency of modern physics is to reduce the whole material universe into waves, and nothing but waves".[10] The idea finds its central expression in this passage, which I incline to take as an epigraph of the play's meaning:

Florizel   What you do
            Still betters what is done. When you speak, sweet,

> I'ld have you do it ever : when you sing,
> I'ld have you buy and sell so, so give alms,
> Pray so; and, for the ord'ring your affairs
> To sing them too : when you do dance, I wish you
> A wave o'th' sea, that you might ever do
> Nothing but that; move still, still so,
> And own no other function : each your doing,
> So singular in each particular,
> Crowns what you are doing in the present deeds,
> That all your acts are queens.
>
> (IV, iv, 135–46)

Perdita, the incarnation of the timeless principle, is visioned as a model or pattern. She expresses the linked metaphors of wave and dance; "wave" is a kind of model in itself, since it is one of a series. More, the essence of "wave" is caught very remarkably in the epizeuxis "move still, still so". Of course "still" means "continually", but there remains the underlying adjectival sense of "at rest". "Move still, still so" conveys the steady momentum of waves, apparently unchanging in themselves and in their relation to each other, yet always in motion. And it is impossible, if one speaks the lines, to inflect each "still" in precisely the same way. There is change within repetition even here. The phrase is a stylistic metaphor for the whole.

III

With *wave* comes, as an alternate term, *dance*. I propose it as the metaphor for the larger movements within time in *The Winter's Tale*. The idea is acknowledged in the pastoral scene. Florizel, in the passage I have cited, links wave and dance : "When you dance, I wish you / A wave o'th'sea . . ." *Dance* becomes the manifest gesture of the stage in IV, iv, as the rustics fall to their festivity. I think it reasonable to term it, as Northrop Frye does, a "masque scene";[11] and this, not because of the loose sense that dancing takes place, but because it is organized into two episodes. First comes the *dance of Shepherds and Shepherdesses,* then follows the *dance of twelve satyrs.* This latter corresponds of course to the anti-masque : thus there is a deeper, more ritually organized sense of courtly dance than is immediately apparent on stage.

This scene is the apotheosis of the dance; and for a general

explication, one need look no further than Sir John Davies'
Orchestra (1596). This poem is not, so far as I know, regarded as
a source for *The Winter's Tale;* it is usual to treat it, as Tillyard
does, as part of the general background of ideas with which all
educated Elizabethans were familiar.[12] Tillyard cites the poem as
"the perfect epitome of the universe seen as dance", and links it,
suggestively, with *A Midsummer Night's Dream.*[13] Still, some of
the lines in *Orchestra* seem especially apt to *The Winter's Tale,*
and one wonders how far Shakespeare had brooded upon, and
assimilated, the poem. Thus:

> Since when they still are carried in a round,
> And changing come one in anothers place,
> Yet doe they neyther mingle nor confound,
> But every one doth keepe the bounded space
> Wherein the daunce doth bid it turne or trace:
> This wondrous myracle did Love devise,
> For Dauncing is Loves proper exercise.
>
> (18)

"And changing come one in anothers place" states the exchange of
roles idea, one that we shall see is central to *The Winter's Tale.*
Then:

> How justly then is Dauncing termed new
> Which with the world in point of time begun?
> Yea Time it selfe (whose birth *Jove* never knew
> And which indeed is elder then the Sun)
> Had not one moment of his age outrunne
> When out leapt Dauncing from the heape of things,
> And lightly rode upon his nimble wing.
> Reason hath both their pictures in her Treasure,
> Where *Time the measure of all moving is;*
> And Dauncing is a moving all in measure:
> Now if you doe resemble that to this
> And think both one, I think you think, amis:
> But if you judge them twins, together got,
> And Time first borne, your judgment erreth not.
>
> (22–33)

Time and all its divisions, as Tillyard says,[14] are a dance. **And:**

For loe the *Sea* that fleets about the Land,
And like a girdle clips her solide wast,
Musick and measure both doth understand :
For his great Christall eye is alwayes cast
Up to the Moone, and on her fixed fast.
And as she daunceth in her pallid spheere,
So daunceth he about the Center heere.

(49)

The sea, with its "proud greene waves in order set" (50), is the great instrument and chronometer of Time in *The Winter's Tale,* as generally in Shakespeare. There is even the suggestion that "These dangerous unsafe *lunes i'th'king"* (II, ii, 30) are the response to the monthly pull of sea and moon. In the larger perspective of the play, Leontes' jealousy is no more than a passing plague, something that will yield to the movement of time. The sea, then, with its regular and stately motion, enacts its part in the universal dance. It influences and figures all human movements. And these movements, considered as part of a dance, take on the aspect of exchange of parts, or roles.

IV

Exchange of roles : that is a recurring characteristic of *The Winter's Tale*. It is much more than the necessary consequence of the structural parallels between Part One and Part Two, which have been noted often enough.[15] Consider the major instances. Polixenes opens I, ii by protesting his wish to leave Bohemia; in IV, ii Polixenes presses Camillo to stay in Bohemia and not return to Sicily. The unwilling guest has become the importunate host. Similarly, Polixenes is the fugitive of Part One and the pursuer of Part Two. Then, the tyrant role of Leontes is transferred to Polixenes in the second half. (This is purely a transference of function. In human terms there is no real comparison between the two, and Shakespeare writes in a convincing psychological explanation for Polixenes' exasperation over Florizel.) The victim becomes the tyrant. Again, it is Polixenes who sustains a gay, courtly inquisition from Hermione in I, ii. It is a miniature trial, and he answers :

Had we pursued that life,
And our weak spirits ne'er been higher rear'd

> With stronger blood, we should have answer'd heaven
> Boldly "not guilty," the imposition clear'd
> Hereditary ours.
>
> (I, ii, 71–5)

Later, Hermione is to exchange the role of prosecutor for defendant, and in her arraignment pleads "not guilty" (III, ii, 27). Leontes, the judge in Act III, concludes the play by seeking from his victims "both your pardons" (v, iii, 147).

Again, the young Florizel is in the beginning the greatest single comfort to his father. He has a variety of parts :

> *Polixenes*   He's all my exercise, my mirth, my matter,
> Now my sworn friend and then mine enemy,
> My parasite, my soldier, statesman, all :
> He makes a July's day short as December,
> And with his varying childness cures in me
> Thoughts that would thick my blood.
>
> (I, ii, 166–71)

Florizel's central role is life-bringing, restorative. In Act IV he is Polixenes' plague, "Kings are no less unhappy, their issue not being gracious" (IV, ii, 29–30). When Polixenes in effect disowns Florizel, "Mark your divorce, young sir, / Whom son I dare not call; thou art too base / To be acknowledged" (IV, iv, 427–9), he puts up a close parallel to Leontes' doubts about Mamillius, "Art thou my boy?" (I, ii, 118) Perdita moves from the "bastard" of Act II to the princess of the conclusion. In the pastoral scene she, a shepherdess, enacts the role of a goddess, and the imagery cunningly asserts her regality and divinity : "no shepherdess, but Flora" (IV, iv, 2) : "Most goddess-like prank'd up" (IV, iv, 10) : "all your acts are queens" (IV, iv, 146) : "she is / The queen of curds and cream" (IV, iv, 160–1).

The exchange of roles is, for the characters, the fundamental movement in time, and their fundamental experience. Guest and host, blessing and curse, prosecutor and defendant, victim and tyrant, subject and ruler : each of the main characters moves through a variety of roles, often directly opposed. The natural opposition between Part One and Part Two does not account for all these shifts. And in this movement from one position to another, we sense a grander metaphor, intimated but just beyond the reach of normal apprehension: the dance. In the exchange of places we intuit a grave and courtly minuet, a dance to the music of time.

v

The exchange of roles leads up to, but does not properly account for, the ultimate structural alternation in *The Winter's Tale*: that of Leontes with Autolycus. This pairing is a separate case, to be judged on its own terms. There is no obvious or immediate relation between Leontes and Autolycus, yet Shakespeare rests on them his entire comic structure.

The fact from which all follows is that they are never on stage together. Now this is not to be discussed in the usual terms of stage doublings. There is no tradition in the theatre of a Leontes and Autolycus doubling, feasible—just—though it is. (The doubling would throw a great burden on the actor. And there is an awkward transition when Autolycus ends Act iv and Leontes begins Act v.) We do not here have a case akin to *King Lear,* where Cordelia's and the Fool's messages to Lear may be reinforced by the physicality of the same actor. The relationship between Leontes and Autolycus has to be approached from a different angle. The New Arden editor throws out a suggestive hint: Autolycus "serves as a faint rhythmic parallel to the evil in Leontes in the first half of the play".[16] He distinguishes, naturally, between the degrees of ill-doing. Leontes is "enveloped in black madness", while "the crimes of Autolycus are hardly felony at all; they are primarily tricks . . .".[17] Joan Hartwig has taken the matter further, and discusses the Leontes–Autolycus relationship through "parody", by which she understands the Greek sense of "parode", "a song sung beside or against the central action".[18] For her, the usual sense of "ridicule" in parody is reduced or excluded, and thus she sees the second element—Autolycus after Leontes—as imitation with contrast, rather than direct burlesque.

From this angle, Joan Hartwig finds several parallels between Leontes and Autolycus. Not all of them are equally convincing, but she is surely right that "Autolycus is both his own attacker and victim [in iv, iii]; so is Leontes."[19] (*Autolycus* means "self-wolf".) Again, Leontes' sexual fantasies parallel the sexual preoccupations of Autolycus' ballads, with their "delicate burthens of dildos and fadings, 'jump her and thump her' ", plackets and cod-pieces, and the appalling fate of the woman who "was turned into a cold fish for she would not exchange flesh with one that loves her" (IV, iv, 283–4). Autolycus cheerfully animates the visions that destroy Leontes. In sum, "Autolycus thus absorbs some of the dis-ordering aspects of Leontes' disturbed imagination from the first half of the play; and, by containing disorder through comic in-consequence, he provides an undersong which contrasts with and makes more credible Leontes' release from false illusion".[20]

"Undersong" will do well enough to fix the idea of relationship; but we can take the matter much further. Consider the linguistic identity of the two. Now the characteristic of Leontes, that finger-print which gives individuality and definition to his speeches, is repetition. It is a tic. I offer here not an exhaustive list of illustra-tions, merely a selection. "But not for joy, not joy" (I, ii, 111). "Come, captain, / We must be neat; not neat, but cleanly, captain" (I, ii, 122–3). ". . . false / As o'er-dyed blacks, as wind, as waters, false / As dice . . ." (I, ii, 131–3). "Go to, go to" (I, ii, 182). "Go, play, boy, play . . . Go, play, boy, play . . ." (I, ii, 187–90). "And his pond fish'd by his next neighbour, by / Sir Smile, his neighbour . . ." (I, ii, 195–6). "Is this nothing? / Why, then the world and all that's in't is nothing : / The covering sky is nothing; Bohemia nothing; / My wife is nothing; nor nothing have these nothings, / If this be nothing" (I, ii, 292–7). "You lie, you lie" (I, ii, 299). "The shrug, the hum or ha . . . these shrugs, these hums and ha's" (II, i, 71, 74). "I have said / She's an adultress; I have said with whom" (II, i, 87–8). "Those of your fact are so—so past all truth" : (III, ii, 86).

These repetitions combine to form a single characteristic, and they denote a mental quality : obsession. There is a crazed assertiveness apparent in many of these instances. Leontes *wills* a belief to be the objective truth, and he seeks to impose that will on all the phenomena that challenge him. Repetition is mere asser-tion. Moreover, it is a trap. Leontes cannot get out of the mental state in which he is condemned to suffer. In all this, he stands in a certain relation with time. He is fixed in a sterile, unmoving present, a present incapable either of change or contented accept-ance. "And many a man there is, *even at this present* . . ." (I, ii, 192). "Nor night nor day no rest" (II, iii, 1) is the key statement of a present from which there is no escape, a nightmare of non-movement. It is like a faulty record over which the stylus moves endlessly on the same revolution. Repetition *without* change, then, is the deepest offence against time. It is characterized by Camillo:

> you may as well
> Forbid the sea for to obey the moon
> As or by oath remove or counsel shake
> The fabric of his folly, whose foundation
> Is pil'd upon his faith and will continue
> The standing of his body.
>
> (I, ii, 426–31)

The great model of time, rhythmic movement, presents itself as the law which Leontes infringes.

Autolycus has a similar way with words. It is a much smaller part, and the opportunities correspondingly fewer, but one can make out a fair case. Here are his repetitions: "A prize! a prize!" (IV, iii, 31–2). "O, help me, help me! pluck but off these rags; and then death, death!" (IV, iii, 55–6). "A footman, sweet sir, a footman" (IV, iii, 68). "O, good sir, softly, good sir!" (IV, iii, 75). "Softly, dear sir; good sir, softly" (IV, iii, 80–1). "No, good sweet sir; no, I beseech you, sir" (IV, iii, 84). "Very true, sir; he, sir, he" (IV, iii, 110). "No, good-faced sir; no, sweet sir" (IV, iii, 123).

There's an ingratiating quality about Autolycus' repetitions. It is a tactic of rhetoric, a policy of reassurance to his victim. He too is fixed in a present,[21] one secure against the past and future. Autolycus has evidently been fired from Florizel's service, and has to contemplate the terrors of "beating and hanging", but "for the life to come, I sleep out the thought of it" (IV, iii, 31). He has come to terms with his present existence. And Autolycus' repetitions take on a curiously apt form, for they are extended into his songs. "Jog on, jog on" (IV, iii, 132). "Come buy of me; come; come buy, come buy" (IV, iv, 230). And a tiny insistence:

Autolycus   Neither.
Dorcas   What, neither?
Autolycus   Neither.
> (IV, iv, 311)

Since virtually all songs make use of the principle of repetition in some form or other, I don't propose to erect a critical monument on this site. Still, the songs do seem particularly well suited to

Autolycus. They take to the point of harmlessness the characteristic so dangerous with Leontes, and ambivalent, if beguilingly so, in Autolycus' fooling of the Clown. Autolycus' songs sublimate, if you like a destructive tendency visible from the play's beginnings.

Grant, then, the parallels of identity between Leontes and Autolycus, and thus their subterranean kinship, how should we regard the pairing? A provisional sense of Autolycus is already available. He reassures, renders harmless, exorcizes. He names and enacts those things which in Leontes cause intense agony, and removes their power to harm. He is restorative, antitoxic.[22] Now Autolycus is not in any sense a model, and he is not even, in general terms, benign. He is benign only in relation to Leontes (and the play as a whole, founded as it is on Leontes' mental collapse). Let us postulate Leontes and Autolycus as divided halves of the same mind. What the one suffers, the other enacts, enjoys, and thus heals. It is the business of *The Winter's Tale* to stage a profound act of psychic reintegration, the re-ordering of pain and loss. And in this movement Leontes and Autolycus are linked : the impulses of one are therapy for the other.

VI

All the same, this account of Leontes and Autolycus is incomplete, since it omits their archetypal opposition : and laughter. When all is done, Leontes is a Tyrant, and Autolycus a comic Rogue. "Comedy", as Daniel Gerould remarks, "thrives on tyranny."[23] The comic spirit is the natural assailant of the all-powerful political tyrant, a pairing with which Gerould's discussion is primarily concerned. More broadly, tyranny is a traditional element of comedy, if the definition widens to include the *senex,* and the despots (parent, husband) of domestic life.[24] Neither approach seems appropriate here. One can scarcely discuss Leontes in terms of *Richard III*—paranoia, but not megalomania ("the two poles between which the dictator oscillates")[25] characterizes him. As Leontes says, rightly, to Paulina, "Were I a tyrant, / Where were her life? She durst not call me so, / If she did know me one" (II, iii, 122–4). Leontes is to tyranny what Richard III is to kingship, not quite there. Nor can one see Leontes simply as a blocking figure, a jealous husband; he is the *subject* of a profoundly original drama, not the mechanism of a conventional piece. But the tension between this quasi-tyrant and the comic spirit is at the heart of the play.

Laughter is the life-force of *The Winter's Tale*. Its coming is signalled so early as II, i, when Leontes' peroration to the courtiers:

> Come, follow us;
> We are to speak in public, for this business
> Will raise us all.

is followed by Antigonus' aside, which terminates the scene:

> To laughter, as I take it,
> If the good truth were known.
> (II, i, 196–9)

A neat anti-climax, this, and in a sense it is true that comedy is anti-climactic to tragedy. Laughter takes shape in II, iii. Leontes apprehends it as his enemy: "Camillo and Polixenes / Laugh at me, make their pastime my sorrow; / They should not laugh if I could reach them . . ." (II, iii, 23–5), and it begins to form around the encounter of Leontes and Paulina. Leontes appears as a mere impotent tyrant, unable to silence Paulina or get her removed, and he makes the rhetorical mistake of calling upon a stereotype of comedy, "Dame Partlet" (II, iii, 75). Paulina, the bearer of the child, and of the life-force itself, scolds him out of countenance. The stealthy advance of the comic spirit is visible here; it retreats before the agonies of Act III; then it reappears, most strangely and indecorously, around the death of Antigonus.

Exit, pursued by a bear. It cannot be other than funny, this shambling, grotesque apparition. The elements in the audience's reaction are hard to analyse; and the death of poor Antigonus is no laughing matter. But it becomes so. Laughter is the principle of indecorum, an audible and visible paradox here. It is the first sign of the coming reassurance that life renews itself. More, the bear has an extra significance that does not emerge until later. "Though authority be a stubborn bear, yet he is oft led by the nose with gold" says the Clown to Autolycus (IV, iv, 830–1). The association of *authority* with *bear* is at least interesting. The bear is the result if not the agent of Leontes' orders. May we not see the bear as figuring the impulse of ridicule directed against the tyrant?

Laughter resumes its course, again indecorously, with the Clown's account of "how the bear tore out his shoulder-bone",[26] and of the drowning of the mariners: "how the poor souls roared, and the sea mocked them; and how the poor gentleman roared, and the bear mocked him . . ." (III, iii, 96–103). The placing of laughter here is exact, since it arrives together with the *waves* of the sea. The way is now prepared for Autolycus and the overt comedy of the second half. Indeed, Autolycus' first song contains subliminal hints of a new King, who can only have overthrown the old Tyrant. "For the red blood *reigns* in the winter's pale . . . For a quart of ale is a dish for a *king*." Laughter, then, comes in like a tide, breaking in upon the tragic action and eventually overwhelming it. It is the advance guard of the challenge to the Tyrant.

And the Tyrant's claims are refuted in the latter stages. Leontes himself experiences both penitence and redemption. His very typology has been shattered. And more than anyone else, Autolycus has achieved it. I find nothing more interesting here than Autolycus' catalogue of horrors:

> He has a son, who shall be flayed alive; then 'nointed over with honey, set on the head of a wasp's nest; then stand till he be three quarters and a dram dead; then recovered again with aqua-vitae or some other hot infusion; then, raw as he is, and in the hottest day prognostication proclaims, shall he be set against a brick-wall, the sun looking with a southward eye upon him, where he is to behold him with flies blown to death.
>
> (IV, iv, 811–19)

It recalls Paulina's:

> What studied torments, tyrants, hast for me?
> What wheels? racks? fires? what flaying? boiling?
> In leads or oils? what old or newer torture
> Must I receive . . .?
>
> (III, ii, 176–9)

And Polixenes, also:

> I'll have thy beauty scratch'd with briers, and made
> More homely than thy state . . .
> I will devise a death as cruel for thee
> As thou are tender to't.
>
> (IV, iv, 435–6, 450–1)

The Tyrant's tortures are real, if verbal, possibilities. Autolycus exorcizes them, makes them vain gestures, objects of derision. The laughter of Autolycus is the surest clue to the challenge to tyranny, and time, in *The Winter's Tale*.

Everything that happens in *The Winter's Tale* becomes a strategy for defining time, and for solacing ourselves in time. The slow, rocking waves of the play intimate the rhythms of time. The rhythms take on the aspect of a dance, the structuring metaphor for the exchange of roles. The shift from one role to its opposite teaches the audience to participate in, and submit to, this dance of humanity. The social enemy, the tyrant, is exposed and overthrown by laughter. In the direction of that laughter, we sense a larger identification between Leontes and a higher order of tyranny. Through Autolycus pulses the life-force that "makes war upon that bloody tyrant, Time".

Notes

References are to *The Complete Works of Shakespeare,* edited by Hardin Craig and David Bevington (Glenview, Ill., 1973).

CHAPTER 1: 2 HENRY VI: TRIAL BY COMBAT

1. E. M. W. Tillyard, *Shakespeare's History Plays* (New York: Barnes & Noble, 1964) p. 175.
2. Ibid., pp. 174, 188. Don M. Ricks accepts Tillyard's line, that "The general theme is again civil dissension", which is displayed through a "masterfully constructed plot". *Shakespeare's Emergent Form: A Study of the Structures of the Henry VI Plays* (Logan, Utah: Utah State University Press, 1968) p. 67.
3. Tillyard, p. 174. "Episodic" is also Robert Ornstein's judgement. See *A Kingdom for a Stage* (Cambridge, Mass.: Harvard University Press, 1972) p. 149.
4. *The Second Part of King Henry VI*, A. S. Cairncross (ed.) (London: Methuen, 1962) pp. li–lii.
5. Irving Ribner, *The English History Play in the Age of Shakespeare* (London: Methuen, 1965) p. 95.
6. In the most notable production of modern times, *The Wars of the Roses* (directed by Peter Hall and John Barton for the Royal Shakespeare Company in 1963/64), the anguish of Henry (David Warner) here was perhaps the most piercing, and central experience of the play.
7. J. P. Brockbank emphasizes the "lynch-law" aspect of this episode, and points out that Say, as the humane judge, corresponds to Gloucester in the pattern. "The Frame of Disorder: *Henry VI*" in *Early Shakespeare,* John Russell Brown and Bernard Harris (eds.) (London: Edward Arnold, 1961) p. 88.

CHAPTER 2: WOMAN AS FOOL: DRAMATIC MECHANISM IN SHAKESPEARE

1. See especially Juliet Dusinberre, *Shakespeare and the Nature of Women* (London and New York: Macmillan and Harper & Row, 1975).
2. See Ralph Berry, Introduction to *Shakespeare's Comedies: Explorations in Form* (Princeton: Princeton University Press, 1972).
3. Talbot was cut completely from the celebrated Hall/Barton adapta-

tion, staged as *The Wars of the Roses* by the Royal Shakespeare Company (RSC) in 1963. He was not missed.

4. The best account of the play that I know is Sigurd Burckhardt's, in *Shakespearean Meanings* (Princeton: Princeton University Press, 1968). "The mode of *I Henry VI* seeks, in fact compels the seeking of, the fullest self-assertion at every moment; it is impatient of indirection, refuses to sacrifice immediate effects for long-range gains . . . it always 'goes for broke' " (p. 54).

5. "The disorder in the world of *Henry VI* is not so much a rupture, a break in the chain of ordered being; it is a disease, an infection endemic in the all-too-pure, all-too-ceremonial lily that makes the noble flower smell far worse than weeds." Ibid., p. 76.

6. So accustomed is the reader to the theatrical domination of Richard that one may not realize what an opportunity this episode (cut from Olivier's film) is to the actress. The RSC production of 1963, later made into a TV version, permanently demonstrates how the actress can dominate the scene. And this is so, because in iv, iv, Queen Elizabeth becomes the moral centre of the drama.

7. Randolph Quirk, "Shakespeare and the English Language", in *A New Companion to Shakespeare Studies*, Kenneth Muir and S. Schoenbaum (eds.) (Cambridge: Cambridge University Press, 1971) p. 70.

8. Ibid., p. 71.

9. See C. T. Onions, *A Shakespeare Glossary*, 2nd edn. (Oxford: The Clarendon Press, 1919).

10. This is, of course, the polar opposite of the "thou" of anger, which Lear adopts in the passage beginning "But goes thy heart with this? . . . thy truth, then, be thy dower!" (i, i, 107, 110). As G. L. Brook remarks, "There is no contradiction between the friendly and hostile uses of *thou.*" G. L. Brook, *The Language of Shakespeare* (London: André Deutsch, 1976) p. 74.

11. Dusinberre, op. cit., p. 114.

CHAPTER 3: HAMLET: NATIONHOOD AND IDENTITY

1. Alvin Kernan, "Place and Plot in Shakespeare", *Yale Review*, 67 (October 1977) 48–56.

2. I have analysed this in *The Shakespearean Metaphor* (London: Macmillan, 1978) pp. 33–6.

3. Fully justified, apparently. Fynes Moryson pays the Danes this mark of respect: "To conclude, the Danes passe (if it be possible) their neighbour Saxons in the excess of their drinking." Fynes Moryson, *An Itinerary* (London 1617) Part iii, Book 2, Chapter 4, p. 101. I quote from the reprint published by Da Capo Press (Theatrum Orbis Terrarum Ltd., Amsterdam and New York, 1971). For an account of what the average Elizabethan knew (or thought he knew) about Denmark, see Martin Holmes, *The Guns of Elsinore* (London: Chatto & Windus, 1964) pp. 46–53.

4. This is not the place for a prolonged examination of the Oedipal

question. The importance of the Gertrude–Hamlet relationship has generally been exaggerated by the commentators, and in current criticism takes up less space than it used to. At the play's end, the Queen seems almost an irrelevance, as Hamlet takes on his father's mode.

5. Webster offers a parallel at the beginning of *The Duchess of Malfi.* In the opening motto-theme, a Prince's court is compared with a fountain:

> but if't chance
> Some curs'd example poison't near the head,
> *Death, and diseases through the whole land spread.*

John Webster, *The Duchess of Malfi,* John Russell Brown (ed.) (London: Methuen, 1964) i, i, 13–15.

6. Northrop Frye, *Fools of Time: Studies in Shakespearean Tragedy* (Toronto: University of Toronto Press, 1967) p. 95.

7. Naturally, I accept the Q1 stage direction *Hamlet leapes in after Leartes,* which seems to me an absolute necessity of symbolism.

8. See John Dover Wilson's note to the passage cited, in his New Cambridge edition of *Hamlet,* 2nd edn. (Cambridge: Cambridge University Press, 1936) p. 239.

9. Neither F nor Q2 mentions the guard in the stage direction for the Court entrance. Still, the Folio identifies "guard" as part of the Court entrance in iii, ii for the play scene. *Prima facie,* the presence of the guards seems less warranted in the play scene, unless one argues that the King requires some protection among a company of foreign actors. By Act v, Hamlet is obviously a dangerous man, and the atmosphere of a fencing match is congruent with a military guard. Perhaps Shakespeare wished to make the non-action of the Court more plausible; and Hamlet, crying "ho! let the door be lock'd" (v, ii, 322) effectively excludes intervention by the Switzers.

10. The best survey of the Danish political system in *Hamlet* is by E. A. J. Honigmann, "The Politics in *Hamlet* and 'The World of the Play'", in *Hamlet,* Stratford-upon-Avon Studies 5, John Russell Brown and Bernard Harris (eds.) (London: Edward Arnold, 1963) pp. 129–47. For Honigmann, "One might almost say that through the momentary indecision of the courtiers the audience glimpses 'the Danish election', for they hold back partly because in doubt as to who is or should be king" (p. 144).

11. Maynard Mack, "The World of *Hamlet*", *Yale Review,* 41 (1952) 510.

12. Avi Erlich, *Hamlet's Absent Father* (Princeton: Princeton University Press, 1977) p. 104.

13. The reference is to John D. Jump's edition of *Doctor Faustus* (London: Methuen, 1965).

14. I quote from the unpublished chapters of Fynes Moryson's *Itinerary,* which appeared in *Shakespeare's Europe,* Charles Hughes (ed.) (London: 1903; reprinted New York: Benjamin Blom, 1967) p. 306.

15. Wilson, *Hamlet,* pp. li–lii.

16. A. C. Bradley, *Shakespearean Tragedy* (London: Macmillan, 1904)

pp. 341–4. I accept the general force of Bradley's argument in his Note B, but not, as will be seen, that of paragraph 4 on the identity of "the city".

17. I do not know that a possible background for Hamlet's "My tables—meet it is I set it down" (I, v, 107) has been remarked. It is from Fynes Moryson's unpublished account (cited above), of Wittenberg:

> For the Students of Germany have little learning from private reading, but take the most part therof upon trust (or hearesay) from the lectures of these grave Professors who dictate theire Lectures with a slowe and tretable voyce, which they write out word by word, their many penns sounding like a great shower of rayne, and if the Professor utter any thing so hastily that the Students cannot write it, they knock upon the Deskes till he repeate it agayne more tretably.
> (*Shakespeare's Europe*, p. 308)

18. Peter Alexander, *Hamlet Father and Son* (Oxford: The Clarendon Press, 1955) p. 35.

19. C. T. Onions, *A Shakespeare Glossary*, 2nd edn. (Oxford: The Clarendon Press, 1919). Gunnar Sjögren points out that Shakespeare shared a popular misconception: "Dansker" meant "a native of Dantzig", not a Dane. "The Danish Background to *Hamlet*", *Shakespeare Studies*, 4 (1968) 223.

20. E. A. J. Honigmann, *Shakespeare: Seven Tragedies: The Dramatist's Manipulation of Response* (London: Macmillan, 1976) p. 70.

21. Ibid., p. 71. The relationship between fencing and duelling is present, yet undefined in this play. S. P. Zitner argues that "in *Hamlet* the duellist's code is made accessible to us", in "Hamlet, Duellist", *University of Toronto Quarterly*, 39 (1969) 16. The duellist's code is unquestionably part of Hamlet's mental background—and, on occasion, foreground. Yet one has to point out that Hamlet does not, in fact, fight a duel. He engages in a fencing match with buttoned foils; this turns into a brawl, with the unbuttoned foil transferred to Hamlet; finally, Hamlet stabs the unarmed Claudius. None of these three phases corresponds to the contours of "duel". "Duel" is a metaphor, not a literal.

22. Dover Wilson (*Hamlet*, p. 183) is emphatic that Hamlet's reference to "French falconers" (II, ii, 450) is not a sneer at the French.

23. Hughes, *Shakespeare's Europe*, p. 75.

24. The Polish connection continues to surface in odd ways. It used to be thought that there were six copies only of the Second Quarto in existence, symmetrically divided between England and the USA. In the 1950s a seventh copy turned up, in excellent condition, in Warsaw Public Library. See *Shakespeare Quarterly*, 11 (1960) 497.

25. For example, by Harry Levin, "Shakespeare's Nomenclature", in *Shakespeare and the Revolution of the Times* (New York: Oxford University Press, 1976) p. 68. Keith Brown detects a possible parallel between Polonius and Ramel (Ramelius), the Danish statesman with a Polish background. See "Polonius, and Fortinbras (and Hamlet?)" *English Studies*, 55 (1974) 218–38.

26. See especially Arthur Wormhoudt, *Hamlet's Mouse Trap: A Psycho-analytical Study of the Drama* (New York: Philosophical Library, 1956) pp. 79–86: Erlich, op. cit., pp. 112–15.
27. Keith Brown finds in *Hamlet* a "double centre" (iii, ii and iv). See " 'Form and Cause Conjoin'd': *Hamlet* and Shakespeare's Workshop", *Shakespeare Survey*, 26 (1973) 11–20.
28. Bradley, op. cit., p. 343.
29. Hughes, *Shakespeare's Europe,* p. 304.
30. Ibid.

CHAPTER 4: HIERARCHIC FORMS: LANGUAGE AND STRUCTURE IN MEASURE FOR MEASURE

1. We need not quibble as to whether Mariana's grange is formally situated outside the city limits, or merely in the outskirts.
2. Edwin Wilson (ed.), *Shaw on Shakespeare* (New York: Dutton, 1961) p. 142.
3. His opening line is "Fellow, why dost thou show me thus to th'world?"
4. The tendency crystallizes in two dwellings. Mariana's grange is moated; Angelo's house has a walled garden, outside a vineyard (also walled, since it has a gate). Each entrance has a lock.
5. J. I. M. Stewart, *Character and Motive in Shakespeare* (London: Longman, 1949) p. 108.
6. Eric Partridge, *Shakespeare's Bawdy* (London: Routledge & Kegan Paul, 1968) p. 46.
7. This difficulty is not properly faced up to in E. A. M. Colman's *The Dramatic Use of Bawdy in Shakespeare* (London: Longman, 1974). Its glossary is, however, invaluable.
8. The definition of "sexual" in *Webster's Third New International Dictionary* is simplest: (2b) ". . . relating to the sphere of behaviour associated with libidinal gratification".
9. Sigmund Freud, *Collected Papers* (New York: Basic Books, 1959) ii, 162.
10. J. W. Lever (ed.), *Measure for Measure,* New Arden edn. (London: Methuen, 1965) p. 97.
11. S. Freud, *The Complete Introductory Lectures on Psychoanalysis,* James Strachey (ed.) (New York: Norton, 1966) p. 158.
12. Ibid.
13. This symbolism is cited in Freud, *Complete Introductory Lectures,* p. 157. Colman (op. cit., p. 211) points out that ten columns of quotation and analogue are cited in J. S. Farmer and W. E. Henley, *Slang and its Analogues: Past and Present* (repr. in 3 vols., New York: Kraus Reprint, 1965). Among the most striking parallels in Shakespeare are *Henry V,* iii, vii, 45–72, and *Antony and Cleopatra,* iv, viii, 14–16.
14. Partridge, p. 39.
15. *OED* gives *"privy member* or *members* carnal member: the secret part or parts".
16. There is a useful general discussion in Rolf Soellner, *Shakespeare's*

Patterns of Self-Knowledge (Columbus: Ohio State University Press, 1972) pp. 215–36.

17. See "Problems of Knowing" in Ralph Berry, *Shakespeare's Comedies: Explorations in Form* (Princeton: Princeton University Press, 1972) pp. 154–74.

18. William Empson, *The Structure of Complex Words* (London: Chatto & Windus, 1951) p. 284.

19. Lever, op. cit., p. 18.

20. This element, to my observation, has been increasingly played up in recent stage productions, notably in Jonathan Miller's *Measure for Measure* at the Greenwich Theatre, 1975.

21. W. K. Wimsatt (ed.), *Samuel Johnson on Shakespeare* (New York: Hill & Wang, 1960).

22. The *locus classicus* of this view is G. Wilson Knight's *"Measure for Measure* and the Gospels", in *The Wheel of Fire*, 4th edn. (London: Methuen, 1949) pp. 73–96.

23. A view advanced (but not endorsed) by Nevill Coghill in "Comic Form in *Measure for Measure*", *Shakespeare Survey*, 8 (1955) 15.

24. Brian Vickers, *The Artistry of Shakespeare's Prose* (London: Methuen, 1968) p. 327.

25. See, Ben Jonson, *Works,* C. H. Herford and Percy and Evelyn Simpson (eds.) 11 vols. (Oxford: The Clarendon Press, 1925–52) i, 142.

26. Hanns Sachs, "The Measure in *Measure for Measure*", *The American Imago,* 1 (1939-40) 80.

27. This is true of John Barton's production (RSC 1969); Keith Hack (RSC, 1974); Jonathan Miller (Greenwich, 1975); and Robin Phillips (Stratford, Ontario, 1975). Three of these productions left Isabella in a state of more or less anguished doubt; one (Miller's) made it plain beyond doubt that Isabella has rejected the Duke.

28. Richard Hosley, "The Playhouses", *The Revels History of Drama in English*, vol. iii: *1576–1613* (London: Methuen, 1975) pp. 193–5.

CHAPTER 5: PATTERN IN OTHELLO

1. See G. Wilson Knight, "The *Othello* Music", *The Wheel of Fire* (London: Methuen, 1965) pp. 91–119.

2. Irving Ribner, *Patterns in Shakespearean Tragedy* (London: Methuen, 1964) pp. 91–115.

3. Bernard Spivack, *Shakespeare and the Allegory of Evil* (New York: Columbia University Press, 1958).

4. G. Wilson Knight, *Principles of Shakespearean Production* (London: Faber, 1936) p. 57.

5. The best recent character analysis that I know is E. A. J. Honigmann's "Secret Motives in *Othello*", in *Shakespeare: Seven Tragedies: The Dramatist's Manipulation of Response* (London: Macmillan, 1976) pp. 77–100.

6. John Wain, *The Living World of Shakespeare* (Harmondsworth: Penguin, 1964) p. 139.

7. See John W. Draper, "The Jealousy of Iago", *Neophilologus,* xxv (1939) 50–60; F. P. Rand, "The Over-Garrulous Iago", *Shakespeare Quarterly,* 1 (1950) 155–61; and Kenneth Muir, "The Jealousy of Iago", *English Miscellany,* ii (Rome, 1951) 65–83.

8. Robert B. Heilman, *Magic in the Web: Action and Language in Othello* (Lexington: University of Kentucky Press, 1956) pp. 38–40.

9. See A. C. Bradley, *Shakespearean Tragedy* (London: Macmillan, 1904) pp. 169–94.

10. A. C. Sprague, *Shakespeare and the Audience: A Study in the Technique of Exposition* (Cambridge, Mass.: Harvard University Press, 1935) p. 76.

11. G. L. Kittredge (ed.), *Othello* (Boston: Ginn, 1941) p. x.

12. Quoted in Marvin Rosenberg, *The Masks of Othello* (Berkeley and Los Angeles: University of California Press, 1961) p. 182.

13. Booth, apparently, played these lines in "low, foreboding tones", Rosenberg, op. cit., p. 83.

14. I agree with F. R. Leavis' conclusion: ". . . what we should see in Iago's prompt success is not so much Iago's diabolic intellect as Othello's readiness to respond." F. R. Leavis, "Diabolic Intellect and the Noble Hero", in *The Common Pursuit* (London: Chatto & Windus, 1962) p. 140.

15. Maud Bodkin, *Archetypal Patterns in Poetry* (London: Oxford University Press, 1963) p. 223.

16. Ribner, op. cit., p. 93.

CHAPTER 6: MACBETH: THE SEXUAL UNDERPLOT

1. See, for example, Kenneth Muir's Introduction to the New Arden edition of *Macbeth* (London: Methuen, 1962) p. xxix.

2. Paul A. Jorgensen, *Our Naked Frailties: Sensational Art and Meaning in 'Macbeth'* (Berkeley, Los Angeles, London: University of California Press, 1971) p. 48.

3. Ibid., pp. 47–51.

4. There is an excellent account of the changes in the playing of Lady Macbeth in Carol Carlisle's *Shakespeare from the Greenroom* (Chapel Hill, N.C.: The University of North Carolina Press, 1969) pp. 395–424. Much information is available *passim* in Dennis Bartholomeusz, *Macbeth and the Players* (Cambridge: Cambridge University Press, 1969).

5. D. W. Harding, "Women's Fantasy of Manhood: a Shakespearean Theme", *Shakespeare Quarterly,* 20 (1969) 247. Paul A. Jorgensen draws attention to the association between manhood and valour, and argues (with a primary reference to Falstaff) that "valour" is a sexually charged term. See "Valor's Better Parts", *Shakespeare Studies,* 9 (1976) 141–58.

6. "The least whereof would quell a lover's hope" (*The Two Gentlemen of Verona,* iv, ii, 13).
"Quail, crush, conclude, and quell!" (*A Midsummer Night's Dream,* v, i, 292).

"Either to quell the Dauphin utterly" (*Henry VI, Part One*, I, i, 163). "To quell the rebels and their complices" (*Henry VI, Part Two*, v, i, 212).
Sir Thomas More, in the fragment, has "How order should be quell'd" (Concordance, 1844) line 82.

7. Quoted by Muir, op. cit., p. 63, on the Porter's scene. He does not make the connection with the "quell" of I, vii, 72.

8. *The Changeling*, Patricia Thomson (ed.), New Mermaid edn. (London: Ernest Benn, 1964) III, iv, 137

9. Partridge's two pages on *knock* begin with citations from the sixteenth century. He cites Florio, "*Cunnata*, a woman knocked" (*Worlde of Wordes*, 1598). See Eric Partridge, *A Dictionary of Slang and Unconventional English*, 2 vols., 5th edn. (London: Routledge & Kegan Paul, 1961). An entry from 1560 is given in the older work, J. S. Farmer and W. E. Henley's *Slang and its Analogues: Past and Present* (repr. in 3 vols., New York: Kraus Reprint, 1965). *Key* with sexual implications is generally available in proverbial sayings: Farmer and Henley cite "Lets the man in and the maid out".

10. *Shakespeare's Sonnets:* edited with analytic commentary by Stephen Booth (New Haven and London: Yale University Press, 1977) p. 499.

11. Ibid.

12. Quoted in Muir, op. cit., p. 61.

13. Eric Partridge, *Shakespeare's Bawdy* (London: Routledge & Kegan Paul, 1955) p. 191.

14. Brian Vickers, *The Artistry of Shakespeare's Prose* (London: Methuen, 1968) p. 380.

15. E. A. M. Colman, *The Dramatic Use of Bawdy in Shakespeare* (London: Longman, 1974) p. 205. The passages are:

> *Pandarus*   For, O, love's bow
> Shoots buck and doe:
> The shaft confounds,
> Not that it wounds,
> But tickles still the sore.
> These lovers cry Oh oh! they die!
> Yet that which seems the wound to kill,
> Doth turn oh! oh! to ha! ha! he!
> So dying love lives still:
> Oh! oh! a while, but ha! ha! ha!
> Oh! oh! groans out for ha! ha! ha!
>   (*Troilus and Cressida*, III, i, 125–36)

> *Posthumus*   perchance he spoke not, but
> Like a full-acorn'd boar, a German one,
> Cried 'O!' and mounted;
>   (*Cymbeline*, II, v, 15–7)

16. John Russell Brown, *Shakespeare's Plays in Performance* (Harmondsworth: Penguin, 1969) p. 202.

17. Carlisle, op. cit., p. 420.

18. I cite a few passages from reviews of productions in the 1970s. Of the Birmingham Repertory Company's production in 1972 (directed by Derek Goldby), "Sara Kestelman . . . strongly establishes Lady Macbeth's sensual power over the Thane. . . ." (Charles Lewsen, *The Times,* 17 October 1972).

    Of the RSC production in 1974 (directed by Trevor Nunn), ". . . this is the first time I have seen sexual blackmail playing its proper part in the first murder. Helen Mirren's Lady Macbeth is not only a voluptuous figure but also capable of making the most atrocious action sound like an enchanting game. 'My dearest love', begins her husband back from the war, and it seems minutes before he breaks his embrace to speak the next line. Up to the coronation, Miss Mirren is sex triumphant; afterwards her collapse begins from the sense of being sexually discarded . . ." (Irving Wardle, *The Times,* 30 October 1974). "That success lies in the sexual electricity generated in the play's earlier stages betwen the unfortunate couple. On returning home, the Macbeth of Nicol Williamson is easy prey for her seductive advances . . ." (Michael Coveney, *Plays and Players,* December 1974, 19).

    Of the RSC version in 1976, again directed by Trevor Nunn, with Ian McKellen and Judi Dench in the leading parts: "The meeting between them was orgasmic in movement, and we later remembered the pushing movements of her hips and thighs when she gently but insidiously pulled Duncan into her castle. Macbeth's doubts were as much quelled by a sexually expressed love as by vehement protestation. . . . The general isolation of Macbeth from Lady Macbeth was more telling than is customary because of the sexual rapport emphasized at the beginning" (Gareth Lloyd Evans, "The RSC's *King Lear* and *Macbeth*", *Shakespeare Quarterly,* 28 (1977) 192.)
19. Peter Brook, *The Empty Space* (Harmondsworth: Penguin, 1972) p. 106.

CHAPTER 7: TIMON OF ATHENS

1. A. E. Housman, *Selected Prose,* John Carter (ed.) (Cambridge: Cambridge University Press, 1961) p. 46.
2. *Timon of Athens,* H. J. Oliver (ed.) (London: Methuen, 1963).
3. C. T. Onions, *The Oxford Dictionary of English Etymology* (Oxford: The Clarendon Press, 1966).
4. Reference is to the Signet edition of *The Two Noble Kinsmen,* edited by Clifford Leech (New York: The New American Library, 1966). It is now generally accepted that the early scenes are from Shakespeare's hand. Note also Pistol's "Let us to France, like horse-leeches, my boys, / To suck, to suck, the very blood to suck!" (*Henry V,* ii, iii, 57–8).
5 M. C. Bradbrook, *Shakespeare the Craftsman* (London: Chatto & Windus, 1969) p. 149.
6. Robert Weimann, *Shakespeare and the Popular Tradition in the Theater,* edited by Robert Schwarzt (Baltimore and London: The Johns Hopkins

University Press, 1978) p. 225. "Shakespeare presents this as if the flatterers were eating Timon *himself.*" Wolfgang Clemen, *The Development of Shakespeare's Imagery* (London: Methuen, 1951) p. 169.

7. William Empson points out some of the curious connections between *God* and *dog* in "The English Dog", *The Structure of Complex Words* (London: Chatto & Windus, 1951) pp. 163–4, 167. In his following chapter, "Timon's Dog", he develops the argument that "Shakespeare is both presenting and refusing a set of feelings about *dog* as metaphor, making it in effect a term of praise, which were already in view and became a stock sentiment after the Restoration" (p. 176).

8. Alexander Schmidt, *Shakespeare-Lexicon,* rev. G. Sarrazin, 4th edn. (Berlin and Leipzig, 1923).

9. "Yet there is one symbol that persists throughout both parts of the play and this has important meaning: gold." G. Wilson Knight, *The Wheel of Fire,* 4th edn. (London: Methuen, 1949) p. 233.

10. Caroline Spurgeon, *Shakespeare's Imagery* (Cambridge: Cambridge University Press, 1935) p. 345.

11. I follow the passage as quoted in "The Power of Money in Bourgeois Society", *Economic and Philosophic Manuscripts of 1844* by Karl Marx, edited by Dirk J. Struik (New York: International Publishers, 1964) p. 166. Marx himself quoted the German translation by Dorothea Tieck.

12. Ibid., pp. 167–8.

13. Marx's comments on Timon are cited by Francelia Butler in *The Strange Critical Fortunes of Shakespeare's 'Timon of Athens'* (Ames: Iowa State University Press, 1966) pp. 146, 150 and are discussed by Anne Paolucci, "Marx, Money, and Shakespeare: The Hegelian Core in Marxist Shakespeare-Criticism", *Mosaic,* x/3 (1977) 139–56. Kenneth Muir, after quoting the Marx passage at length, asserts that "It provides an effective commentary on Timon's diatribes about the power of gold and throws a useful sidelight on one aspect of the play." "*Timon of Athens* and the Cash-Nexus", *The Singularity of Shakespeare* (Liverpool: Liverpool University Press, 1977) p. 73. Muir does not in fact analyse *Timon* at all (Alcibiades, for instance, is ignored) and the effectiveness of Marx's commentary has to be inferred. In his conclusion, Muir escapes from Shakespeare to Marx: "Marx uses the quotations from *Timon of Athens* to support his criticisms of an acquisitive society. One might go further and say that some of these criticisms are suggested by Shakespeare, and that Shakespeare was one of the spiritual godparents of the *Communist Manifesto*" (p. 75).

14. Marx, op. cit., p. 169.

15. Alcibiades has not escaped an adverse Press, nevertheless. "Yet Alcibiades, trooping about with his two whores and threatening to destroy his native city, makes rather a poor hero", Ruth Levitsky, "*Timon*: Shakespeare's *Magnyfycence* and an embryonic *Lear*", *Shakespeare Studies,* 11 (1978) 118. No doubt Alcibiades experienced difficulties in persuading the right sort of young lady to accompany him on his campaigns. Marx would have understood.

16. Empson, op. cit., p. 182.

17. E. C. Pettet, *"Timon*: the disruption of feudal morality", *Review of English Studies,* 23 (1947) 321–36.

18. Ibid., 321.

19. Bacon, *Essays,* "Of usury". The best treatment of the usury question is in R. H. Tawney, *Religion and the Rise of Capitalism* (West Drayton, Middlesex: Penguin, 1948). L. C. Knights has a useful note on the subject, in *Drama and Society in the Age of Jonson* (Harmondsworth: Penguin, 1962) pp. 138–41.

20. Winifred Nowottny, "Acts IV and V of *Timon*", *Shakespeare Quarterly,* 10 (1959) 494.

21. Bacon, *Essays,* "Of seditions and troubles".

22. *The Oxford Dictionary of English Proverbs,* 3rd edn., revised by F. P. Wilson (Oxford: The Clarendon Press, 1970). The next three illustrations are taken from it.

23. Ben Jonson, *Works,* C. H. Herford and Percy and Evelyn Simpson (eds.), 11 vols. (Oxford: The Clarendon Press, 1925–52) III, p. 146.

24. Maurice Morgann, "An Essay on the Dramatic Character of Sir John Falstaff", reprinted in Maurice Morgann, *Shakespearean Criticism,* Daniel A. Fineman (ed.) (Oxford: The Clarendon Press, 1972) p. 149.

25. John Gerard, *The Herball or Generall Historie of Plants* (London: 1597) Book III, Chapter 92, p. 1266. The citation is to the reprint in two volumes published by Walter J. Johnson, Inc. (Amsterdam and Norwood, New Jersey: Theatrum Orbis Terrarum Ltd., 1974).

26. The explicit tirades against whores are something else. I agree with A. S. Collins that "Modern critics over-emphasize the element of 'sex nausea'—it is only part of the confusion Timon invokes . . ." "*Timon*: a Reconsideration", *Review of English Studies,* 22 (1946) 105.

27. Oliver, New Arden edn., p. 131.

28. My speculation here is, of course, independent of the theory that two hands were concerned with the copy for *Timon.* This view has been authoritatively canvassed. E. A. J. Honigmann, for instance, sees two compositors. *"Timon of Athens",* *Shakespeare Quarterly,* 12 (1961) 3–20. Oliver thinks that part of the copy was Shakespeare's foul papers, another part a transcript made by Ralph Crane (New Arden edition, pp. xix-xx). These possibilities leave untouched the potential of "Raigne" as word play. J. C. Maxwell, however, takes the apparent meaning of "Raigne" for granted: Timon, for him, leaves the world as a "king manqué". *"Timon",* *Scrutiny,* 15 (1948) 200.

29. Spurgeon details some of the images of sweets (op. cit., p. 199).

30. I agree with the view of *Timon* that sees it as closely linked, in time and thought, with *Coriolanus* and *Antony and Cleopatra.* See Honigmann, op. cit.

CHAPTER 8: THE WINTER'S TALE: A DANCE TO THE MUSIC OF TIME

1. Frederick Turner, *Shakespeare and the Nature of Time* (Oxford: The Clarendon Press, 1971) p. 3.

2. Inga-Stina Ewbank's "The Triumph of Time in *The Winter's Tale*",

Review of English Literature, 5 (April 1964) contains a discussion of the iconography. Time's choric speech is well analysed in Turner, op. cit., pp. 146–61; and in David Young's *The Heart's Forest* (New Haven and London: Yale University Press, 1972) pp. 140–5.

3. This has been accomplished most thoroughly in Ernest Schanzer, "The Structural Pattern of *The Winter's Tale*", *Review of English Literature,* 5 (April 1964).

4. Young, op. cit., p. 134.

5. John Gerard, *The Herball or Generall Historie of Plants* (London, 1597). Citations are to the reprint in two volumes published by Walter J. Johnson, Inc. (Amsterdam and Norwood, New Jersey: Theatrum Orbis Terrarum Ltd., 1974).

6. See J. H. P. Pafford's New Arden edition of *The Winter's Tale* (London: Methuen, 1963) p. 83.

7. *Herball,* iii, p. 1110.

8. *Herball,* ii, p. 1072.

9. "The intermeshed syntaxes by which the two pairs of lines are at once independent of one another and at the same time joined in a third identity that overlies them is such that the physics of the quatrain approximate the physics the quatrain remarks in waves." *Shakespeare's Sonnets,* edited with analytic commentary by Stephen Booth (New Haven and London: Yale University Press, 1977) p. 239.

10. Caroline Spurgeon, *Shakespeare's Imagery* (Cambridge: Cambridge University Press, 1935) p. 305.

11. Northrop Frye, "Romance as Masque", in *Shakespeare's Romances Reconsidered,* Carol McGinnis Kay and Henry E. Jacobs (eds.) (Lincoln and London: University of Nebraska Press, 1978) p. 38.

12. E. M. W. Tillyard, "The Cosmic Dance", in *The Elizabethan World Picture* (Harmondsworth: Penguin, 1963) pp. 123–9. Robert Krueger, while not disagreeing fundamentally with Tillyard's treatment, stresses the "essential levity" and frivolousness of the poem. See Robert Krueger, *The Poems of Sir John Davies* (Oxford: The Clarendon Press, 1975) p. lxiv. The citations that follow are to Krueger's edition.

13. Tillyard, op. cit., p. 126.

14. Ibid.

15. For example, by Schanzer, op. cit.: and Fitzroy Pyle, *The Winter's Tale: A Commentary on the Structure* (London: Routledge & Kegan Paul, 1969) passim.

16. Pafford, op. cit., p. lxxx.

17. Ibid.

18. Joan Hartwig, "Cloten, Autolycus and Caliban: Bearers of Parodic Burdens", in *Shakespeare's Romances Reconsidered,* Carol McGinnis Kay and Henry E. Jacobs (eds.) op. cit., p. 93.

19. Ibid., p. 100.

20. Ibid., p. 101.

21. "The key to Autolycus' character is what he himself calls the 'extempore' nature of his acts. . . . Autolycus . . . lives only in the present." John Taylor, "The Patience of *The Winter's Tale*", *Essays in Criticism,* 23 (1973) 352–3.

22. The metaphor is Tillyard's, but he uses it in a different sense. He sees Autolycus as a corrective to the over-sweetness of the country scene, the Earthly Paradise (*Shakespeare's Last Plays*, London: Chatto & Windus, 1958). I prefer to view Autolycus as antidote to the poison in Leontes.
23. Daniel Gerould, "Tyranny and Comedy", in *Comedy: New Perspectives*, Maurice Charney (ed.) the inaugural issue of *New York Literary Forum* (Spring 1978) 3.
24. This is Northrop Frye territory: see, for instance, his *A Natural Perspective* (New York: Harcourt, Brace & World, 1965) p. 74.
25. Gerould, op. cit., p. 19.
26. As Northrop Frye points out, Part Two opens with Autolycus complaining that his shoulder-blade is out (*A Natural Perspective*, p. 115). Again, Autolycus' message is of reassurance.

Index